CW01433559

88341903R00050

Made in the USA
Las Vegas, NV
06 April 2024

The
HUMAN
RIGHTS
Haggadah

הגדה של פסח

By Shlomo Levin

The website delves into human rights issues currently affecting Israel and the Jewish community to help us better understand both our own views and the views of those who disagree with us.

Visit or scan to continue the conversation.

Dedicated in memory of my father, Jacob Levin,
who continues to inspire me and who made this work possible.

Introduction

This Haggadah highlights human rights issues as they come up in the Passover story. Lines from the traditional text that will be commented on are **enlarged and printed in brown.**

This Haggadah contains three types of boxes:

Yellow from the Rabbis boxes show how Jewish sources address human rights issues.

Blue International Law boxes explain how human rights issues are covered by treaties and declarations.

Dialogue boxes are green, the color of the previous two boxes combined, since they represent human rights interacting with Jewish values. Dialogue boxes explain different viewpoints and end with questions for discussion.

The Human Rights Haggadah

Table of Contents

Bedikat Chametz

בְּדִיקַת חָמֵץ

Searching for Chametz

Recited before searching for chametz
the evening before the holiday:

בָּרוּךְ אַתָּה יְיָ אֱלֹהֵינוּ מֶלֶךְ הָעוֹלָם, אֲשֶׁר קִדְּשָׁנוּ בְּמִצְוֹתָיו, וְצִוָּנוּ עַל בְּעוּר חָמֵץ.

Blessed are you, Lord our God, King of the Universe, who has sanctified us with his commandments and commanded us to destroy chametz.

After the search, recite:

כָּל חֲמִירָא וַחֲמִיעָא דְּאִכָּא בִרְשׁוּתִי דְּלָא חֲמִתֵּה וּדְלָא בְעַרְתֵּה וּדְלָא יְדַעְנָא לֵהּ לִבָּטֵל וְלֶהֱוֵי הֶפְקֵר כְּעַפְרָא דְאַרְעָא.

All chametz in my possession, including chametz I have not found, have no knowledge of, and have been unable to destroy, may it be nullified and ownerless like dust of the earth.

Biur Chametz

בְּעוּר חָמֵץ

Burning the Chametz

Recited the morning before the holiday,
when burning the chametz:

כָּל חֲמִירָא וַחֲמִיעָא דְּאִכָּא בִרְשׁוּתִי דַּחֲזִתֵּה וּדְלָא חֲזִתֵּה, דַּחֲמִתֵּה וּדְלָא חֲמִתֵּה, דְּבִעַרְתֵּה וּדְלָא בְעַרְתֵּה, לִבָּטֵל וְלֶהֱוֵי הֶפְקֵר כְּעַפְרָא דְאַרְעָא.

All chametz in my possession, whether I have seen it, found it, destroyed it or not, may it be nullified and ownerless like dust of the earth.

Hadlakat Nerot

הַדְלָקַת נֵרוֹת

Lighting of the Holiday Candles

If celebrating the seder on Friday night,
add the words in italics.

Blessed are you, Lord our God, King of the Universe, who has sanctified us with his commandments and commanded us to light the candles for *(Shabbat and)* Yom Tov.

בָּרוּךְ אַתָּה יְיָ אֱלֹהֵינוּ מֶלֶךְ הָעוֹלָם, אֲשֶׁר קִדְּשָׁנוּ בְּמִצְוֹתָיו וְצִוָּנוּ לְהַדְלִיק נֵר *(שֶׁל שַׁבָּת וְ)* שֶׁל יוֹם טוֹב.

Blessed are you, Lord our God, King of the Universe, who has kept us in life and enabled us to celebrate this holiday.

בָּרוּךְ אַתָּה יְיָ אֱלֹהֵינוּ מֶלֶךְ הָעוֹלָם, שֶׁהֶחֱיָנוּ וְקִיְּמָנוּ וְהִגִּיעָנוּ לַזְּמַן הַזֶּה.

קַדֵּשׁ Kadesh

וּרְחַץ Urchatz

כַּרְפַּס Karpas

יַחַץ Yachatz

מַגִּיד Magid

רָחְצָה Rachtza

מוֹצִיא מַצָּה Motze Matzah

כּוֹרֵךְ
Korech

מָרוֹר
Maror

שֻׁלְחָן עוֹרֵךְ
Shulchan Orech

בָּרֵךְ
Barech

צָפוּן
Tzafun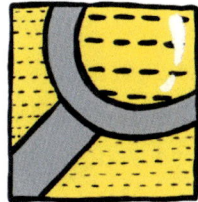

נִרְצָה
Nirtzah

הַלֵּל
Hallel

Kadesh   קַדֵּשׁ

The First Cup

Pour the first cup of wine. We stand for Kiddush.
If celebrating the seder on Friday night,
add the words in italics.

Kiddush   קידוש

*There was evening and there was
morning, the sixth day. The heavens
and the earth and all they contain
was completed. And on the seventh
day God completed the work he had
done, and God rested on the seventh
day from all the work he had done.
And God blessed the seventh day
and made it holy, for on that day
he rested from all his work, all that
God had created to do.*

וַיְהִי עֶרֶב וַיְהִי בֹקֶר יוֹם הַשִּׁשִּׁי.

וַיְכֻלּוּ הַשָּׁמַיִם וְהָאָרֶץ וְכָל־צְבָאָם.

וַיְכַל אֱלֹהִים בַּיּוֹם הַשְּׁבִיעִי מְלַאכְתּוֹ

אֲשֶׁר עָשָׂה וַיִּשְׁבֹּת בַּיּוֹם הַשְּׁבִיעִי מִכָּל

מְלַאכְתּוֹ אֲשֶׁר עָשָׂה. וַיְבָרֶךְ אֱלֹהִים

אֶת יוֹם הַשְּׁבִיעִי וַיְקַדֵּשׁ אוֹתוֹ כִּי

בוֹ שָׁבַת מִכָּל־מְלַאכְתּוֹ אֲשֶׁר בָּרָא

אֱלֹהִים לַעֲשׂוֹת.

Attention, everyone:

Blessed are you, Lord our God, King of the World, creator of the fruit of the vine. Blessed are you, Lord our God, King of the Universe, **who has chosen us from all the nations**, lifted us up from speakers of all the other languages, and sanctified us with his commandments. Lord our God, give us with love (*Shabbat for rest and*) festivals for joy, holidays for rejoicing. May this (*Shabbat day and*) festival of matzah, the time of our freedom, (*with love*) be a holy day, a remembrance of the exodus from Egypt. **For you have chosen us and you have sanctified us from all the nations.** (*Shabbat*) and holy festivals (*with love and kindness*), joy and rejoicing you have bequeathed to us. Blessed are you, God, who hallows (*the Shabbbat and*) Israel and the holidays.

סַבְרִי מָרָנָן וְרַבָּנָן וְרַבּוֹתַי.

בָּרוּךְ אַתָּה יי, אֱלֹהֵינוּ מֶלֶךְ הָעוֹלָם בּוֹרֵא פְּרִי הַגָּפֶן. בָּרוּךְ אַתָּה יי, אֱלֹהֵינוּ מֶלֶךְ הָעוֹלָם **אֲשֶׁר בָּחַר בָּנוּ מִכָּל עָם** וְרוֹמְמָנוּ מִכָּל לָשׁוֹן וְקִדְּשָׁנוּ בְּמִצְוֹתָיו. וַתִּתֶּן לָנוּ יי אֱלֹהֵינוּ בְּאַהֲבָה (*שַׁבָּתוֹת לִמְנוּחָה וּ*) מוֹעֲדִים לְשִׂמְחָה, חַגִּים וּזְמַנִּים לְשָׂשׂוֹן, (*אֶת יוֹם הַשַּׁבָּת הַזֶּה וְ*) אֶת יוֹם חַג הַמַּצּוֹת הַזֶּה זְמַן חֵרוּתֵנוּ, (*בְּאַהֲבָה*) מִקְרָא קֹדֶשׁ זֵכֶר לִיצִיאַת מִצְרָיִם. **כִּי בָנוּ בָחַרְתָּ** וְאוֹתָנוּ קִדַּשְׁתָּ מִכָּל הָעַמִּים, (*וְשַׁבָּת*) וּמוֹעֲדֵי קָדְשֶׁךָ (*בְּאַהֲבָה וּבְרָצוֹן*) בְּשִׂמְחָה וּבְשָׂשׂוֹן הִנְחַלְתָּנוּ. בָּרוּךְ אַתָּה יי, מְקַדֵּשׁ (*הַשַּׁבָּת וְ*) יִשְׂרָאֵל וְהַזְּמַנִּים.

If celebrating the seder on a Saturday night add here havdallah (found on next page). On all nights continue:

Blessed are you, Lord our God, King of the Universe, who has kept us in life, sustained us, and brought us to this occasion.

בָּרוּךְ אַתָּה יי, אֱלֹהֵינוּ מֶלֶךְ הָעוֹלָם, שֶׁהֶחֱיָנוּ וְקִיְּמָנוּ וְהִגִּיעָנוּ לַזְּמַן הַזֶּה.

We sit and drink the wine while reclining.

Added when celebrating the seder on a Saturday
night. The first blessing is recited while looking at the
holiday candles. No spice box is used.

Havdallah ———————————————— הבדלה

Blessed are you, Lord our God, King of the
world, creator of the light of the fire.
Blessed are you, Lord our God, King of
the World, who distinguishes between
the holy and the mundane. Between
light and darkness, between Israel and
the nations, between the seventh day
and the six days of creation. Between
the holiness of the Shabbat and the
holiness of the holiday you have
distinguished, and you have sanctified
the seventh day from the six days
of creation. You have separated and
made holy your nation Israel with your
holiness. Blessed are you, God, who
distinguishes between levels of holiness.

בָּרוּךְ אַתָּה יי, אֱלֹהֵינוּ מֶלֶךְ הָעוֹלָם,
בּוֹרֵא מְאוֹרֵי הָאֵשׁ.
בָּרוּךְ אַתָּה יי, אֱלֹהֵינוּ מֶלֶךְ הָעוֹלָם
הַמַּבְדִיל בֵּין קֹדֶשׁ לְחֹל, בֵין אוֹר לְחשֶׁךְ,
בֵּין יִשְׂרָאֵל לָעַמִּים, בֵּין יוֹם הַשְּׁבִיעִי
לְשֵׁשֶׁת יְמֵי הַמַּעֲשֶׂה. בֵּין קְדֻשַּׁת שַׁבָּת
לִקְדֻשַּׁת יוֹם טוֹב הִבְדַּלְתָּ, וְאֶת יוֹם
הַשְּׁבִיעִי מִשֵּׁשֶׁת יְמֵי הַמַּעֲשֶׂה קִדַּשְׁתָּ.
הִבְדַּלְתָּ וְקִדַּשְׁתָּ אֶת עַמְּךָ יִשְׂרָאֵל
בִּקְדֻשָּׁתֶךָ. בָּרוּךְ אַתָּה יי, הַמַּבְדִיל בֵּין
קֹדֶשׁ לְקֹדֶשׁ.

Blessed are you, Lord our God, King
of the World, who has kept us in life,
sustained us, and brought us to this
occasion.

בָּרוּךְ אַתָּה יי, אֱלֹהֵינוּ מֶלֶךְ הָעוֹלָם,
שֶׁהֶחֱיָנוּ וְקִיְּמָנוּ וְהִגִּיעָנוּ לַזְּמַן הַזֶּה.

We sit and drink the wine while reclining.

Equality and the Chosen People

"The Chosen People" "אֲשֶׁר בָּחַר בָּנוּ מִכָּל עָם"

Human Rights are Equal for All

Everyone is entitled to all the rights and freedoms set forth in this Declaration, without distinction of any kind, such as race, colour, sex, language, religion, political or other opinion, national or social origin, property, birth or other status.

– Universal Declaration of Human Rights, Article II.

Is the Concept of a Chosen People Compatible with Human Rights?

Mordechai Kaplan, founder of the Reconstructionist movement, rejected the concept of being the chosen people. He said belief in being a chosen people leads to racism, because it implies that the chosen people are superior to others.

Nevertheless, many Jewish thinkers (including some in the Reconstructionist movement itself) continue to embrace the notion of the chosen people. They claim that according to the Torah, Jews are chosen for extra responsibilities, such as spreading ethical teachings or fulfilling the commandments, rather than rights or privileges. In their view, since anyone can convert to Judaism there is no basis for finding a particular race or ethnicity to be superior to others.

Is belief in a chosen people compatible with the principle of equality central to human rights?

Urchatz

וּרְחַץ

Hand Washing.

We pour water from a cup over our fingers to prepare for
eating the karpas. No blessing is said.

Karpas

כַּרְפַּס

Eating Greens

We dip a green vegetable such as parsley or celery in salt
water. Before eating we recite the blessing:

Blessed are you, Lord our God, King of the
Universe, creator of the produce of the earth.

בָּרוּךְ אַתָּה יי, אֱלֹהֵינוּ מֶלֶךְ
הָעוֹלָם, בּוֹרֵא פְּרִי הָאֲדָמָה.

Yachatz

יַחַץ

Breaking the Middle Matzah.

Take the middle matzah from the seder plate and crack it in
half. The larger half is set aside to be the afikoman.
The smaller is saved to be eaten before the meal.

Magid

מַגִּיד

Telling the Passover Story.

Is Food a Human Right?

Ha Lachmha Anyah

This is the bread of affliction that our ancestors ate in Eygpt.
**All who are hungry let them come and eat,
all in need let them join our celebration of Pesach.**
Now we are here, next year may we be in the land of Israel.
This year we are slaves, next year we will be free.

הָא לַחְמָא עַנְיָא

הָא לַחְמָא עַנְיָא דִי אֲכָלוּ אַבְהָתָנָא בְּאַרְעָא דְמִצְרָיִם.

כָּל דִכְפִין יֵיתֵי וְיֵיכֹל,

כָּל דִצְרִיךְ יֵיתֵי וְיִפְסַח.

הָשַׁתָּא הָכָא - לְשָׁנָה הַבָּאָה בְּאַרְעָא דְיִשְׂרָאֵל. הָשַׁתָּא עַבְדֵי - לְשָׁנָה הַבָּאָה בְּנֵי חוֹרִין.

As the Universal Declaration of Human Rights was drafted, the inclusion of food was a major source of disagreement. Some countries, primarily the Soviet Union and Asian nations, argued that economic rights such as food, housing, and employment are most important. It is worth trading political freedoms to ensure economic stability.

Western nations argued that political rights such as freedom of speech, freedom of religion, and participation in government are most important. Western nations didn't see food, health care, and housing as universal rights.

In the end, economic rights were included in the declaration. But even though all human rights are said to be indivisible from one another and equally important, in practice no government can guarantee them all. Western countries have continued to emphasize the political, while other countries prioritize the economic.

From the International Covenant on Economic, Social and Cultural Rights

Article 11:1

The States Parties to the present Covenant recognize the right of everyone to an adequate standard of living for himself and his family, including adequate food, clothing and housing, and to the continuous improvement of living conditions.

This means that governments must make sure food is available for everyone to purchase, without discrimination. Food also must be affordable, meaning that citizens should be able to buy food without having to sacrifice other essential needs.

Explanation of the Office of the High Commissioner for Human Rights, summarized from https://www.ohchr.org/en/food

How Much Does a Poor Person Need?

It is a positive commandment to give tzedakah according to one's ability. . .and we must be very careful about this, because it can even lead to bloodshed, should a beggar die while waiting for his sustenance. . .

How much should we give to a poor person? Whatever he lacks. How? If he is hungry, feed him. If he needs clothing, clothe him. If he has no household utensils, buy them for him. Even if he was accustomed to riding a horse with a servant running before him when he was wealthy, and then he became poor, buy him a horse and a servant. So too for everyone according to their needs.

– Shulchan Aruch (code of Jewish Law) Laws of tzedakah 247:1 and 250:1

Food Compared to Other Rights

One might assume that economic rights, such as access to food, clothing, shelter, and health care, should be just as important as political rights. After all, the right to vote, freedom of expression, freedom of religion, and so on cannot be used unless basic needs are first met.

Then again, economic rights may be particularly difficult for governments to fulfill. To attempt to do so governments may need to micromanage the economy and dictate citizens' jobs and work training, conflicting with personal freedom. There is no easy way to determine what quality of food and health care people must have access to, let alone what is affordable. And if political freedoms are prioritized, that may give citizens the tools to advance their economic interests on their own.

Are economic, civil, and political rights all equal, or should some come before others?

The Four Questions

_____ ?**מַה נִּשְׁתַּנָּה**

Why is this night different from all other nights?

מַה נִּשְׁתַּנָּה הַלַּיְלָה הַזֶּה מִכָּל הַלֵּילוֹת?

On all other nights
we eat chametz and matzo.
Tonight, why do we eat
only matzo?

שֶׁבְּכָל הַלֵּילוֹת
אָנוּ אוֹכְלִין
חָמֵץ וּמַצָּה.
הַלַּיְלָה הַזֶּה כֻּלּוֹ מַצָּה.

On all other nights
we eat any kind of herbs.
Tonight, why do we eat
the bitter herbs?

שֶׁבְּכָל הַלֵּילוֹת
אָנוּ אוֹכְלִין
שְׁאָר יְרָקוֹת
הַלַּיְלָה הַזֶּה מָרוֹר.

On all other nights
we do not dip even once.
Tonight, why do we dip
the greens twice?

שֶׁבְּכָל הַלֵּילוֹת
אֵין אָנוּ מַטְבִּילִין
אֲפִילוּ פַּעַם אֶחָת.
הַלַּיְלָה הַזֶּה שְׁתֵּי פְעָמִים.

On all other nights
we eat sitting or reclining.
Tonight, why do we
all recline?

שֶׁבְּכָל הַלֵּילוֹת
אָנוּ אוֹכְלִין
בֵּין יוֹשְׁבִין וּבֵין מְסֻבִּין.
הַלַּיְלָה הַזֶּה כֻּלָּנוּ מְסֻבִּין.

Modern Slavery

Avadim Hayinu

We were slaves to Pharoah in Egypt. And God took us out from there with a strong hand and outstretched arm. And if God had not redeemed our ancestors from Egypt, then **we, along with our children and all future generations, would still be slaves to Pharoah in Egypt.** Even if we all were wise, all scholarly, all elders, all knowledgeable of the Torah, we would still be required to tell the story of the Exodus. And the more one tells the story, this is to be praised.

עֲבָדִים הָיִינוּ

עֲבָדִים הָיִינוּ לְפַרְעֹה בְּמִצְרָיִם, וַיּוֹצִיאֵנוּ יי אֱלֹהֵינוּ מִשָּׁם בְּיָד חֲזָקָה וּבִזְרֹעַ נְטוּיָה. וְאִלּוּ לֹא הוֹצִיא הַקָּדוֹשׁ בָּרוּךְ הוּא אֶת אֲבוֹתֵינוּ מִמִּצְרָיִם, **הֲרֵי אָנוּ וּבָנֵינוּ וּבְנֵי בָנֵינוּ מְשֻׁעְבָּדִים הָיִינוּ לְפַרְעֹה בְּמִצְרָיִם.** וַאֲפִילוּ כֻּלָּנוּ חֲכָמִים כֻּלָּנוּ נְבוֹנִים כֻּלָּנוּ זְקֵנִים כֻּלָּנוּ יוֹדְעִים אֶת הַתּוֹרָה מִצְוָה עָלֵינוּ לְסַפֵּר בִּיצִיאַת מִצְרָיִם. וְכָל הַמַּרְבֶּה לְסַפֵּר בִּיצִיאַת מִצְרַיִם הֲרֵי זֶה מְשֻׁבָּח:

Westminster, London, UK. October 19th, 2019. Young people gather in London to raise awareness of modern day slavery across the world.

From the International Labor Organization

Forced labor is when persons are coerced to work through the use of violence or intimidation, or by more subtle means such as manipulated debt, retention of identity papers or threats of denunciation to immigration authorities.
This is considered a form of modern slavery.

Source: https://www.ilo.org/global/topics/forced-labour/definition/lang--en/index.htm

The Right to Stop Work

Even if a worker already began to work but changes his mind in the middle of the day he can quit, as it says (Leviticus 25:55) 'The children of Israel are slaves unto me (God)'. This means they are slaves to God only, but not to other humans.

– Maimonides Laws of Hiring 9:4

International Labor Organization on Ending Modern Slavery

Here are highlights of a list of steps the International Labor Organization suggests would help end modern slavery:

- Extend basic income security to all workers, so they will be able to say no to jobs that are abusive and quit jobs that become so.

- Extend collective bargaining to all workers, including those in the informal economy. This way they will be able to advocate for secure and decent work.

- Stop fraudulent recruitment. Traffickers often entice people to leave their countries with promises of good jobs somewhere else. Then, when the workers are vulnerable and indebted in a foreign country, the traffickers trap them in poor conditions.

- Expand government labor inspections. For example, fishing, agriculture, and domestic help are all areas in which modern slavery may be common but governments often fail to inspect.

- Extend special protections to migrants and victims of war and natural disasters, as these groups are especially prone to modern slavery.

Source: ILO Global Estimates of Modern Slavery: Forced Labor and Forced Marriage (pp. 15-17)

Ending Modern Slavery

Allowing masters to keep humans as property has been abolished, but according to the International Labor Organization as of 2022 there were still 27.6 million people working in forced labor. This takes place all around the world, with more than half in upper middle income or high income countries.

Source: https://www.ilo.org/wcmsp5/groups/public/---ed_norm/---ipec/documents/publication/wcms_854795.pdf

When do coercion, threats, low or no wages, and bad working conditions combine to create conditions that should be considered modern slavery?

New York shirtwaist strike of 1909, in which workers (majority of whom were immigrant Jewish women) protested crowded and unsanitary conditions, wages of just a few dollars a day (with women earning less than half of male salaries), and 65+ hour work weeks in textile factories in New York City.

There was an incident involving Rabbi Eliezer, Rabbi Yehoshua, Rabbi Elazar ben Azarya, Rabbi Akiva, and Rabbi Tarphon, who were celebrating the seder in Bnei Brak. They retold the story of the Exodus the entire night, until their students came and said: Rabbis, it is now time to read the morning Shma.

Rabbi Elazar ben Azarya said:

I am like a man of seventy years, but I have never had merit to understand why we recite the paragraph concerning the Exodus in the night time shma (as well as the morning) until Ben Zoma explained it to me. It says in the Torah: In order to remember the day on which you went out from Egypt all the days of your life.

The days of your life would mean the days only,

but **all the days of your life** means during the night time as well.

The sages said:

The days of your life would mean just in this world,

all the days of your life comes to include the days of the mashiach.

מַעֲשֶׂה בְּרַבִּי אֱלִיעֶזֶר וְרַבִּי יְהוֹשֻעַ וְרַבִּי אֶלְעָזָר בֶּן עֲזַרְיָה וְרַבִּי עֲקִיבָא וְרַבִּי טַרְפוֹן שֶׁהָיוּ מְסֻבִּין בִּבְנֵי בְרַק וְהָיוּ מְסַפְּרִים בִּיצִיאַת מִצְרַיִם כָּל אוֹתוֹ הַלַּיְלָה, עַד שֶׁבָּאוּ תַלְמִידֵיהֶם וְאָמְרוּ לָהֶם רַבּוֹתֵינוּ הִגִּיעַ זְמַן קְרִיאַת שְׁמַע שֶׁל שַׁחֲרִית.

אָמַר רַבִּי אֶלְעָזָר בֶּן עֲזַרְיָה:

הֲרֵי אֲנִי כְּבֶן שִׁבְעִים שָׁנָה
וְלֹא זָכִיתִי שֶׁתֵּאָמֵר
יְצִיאַת מִצְרַיִם בַּלֵּילוֹת
עַד שֶׁדְּרָשָׁה בֶּן זוֹמָא,
שֶׁנֶּאֱמַר, לְמַעַן תִּזְכֹּר אֶת
יוֹם צֵאתְךָ מֵאֶרֶץ מִצְרַיִם
כֹּל יְמֵי חַיֶּיךָ.
יְמֵי חַיֶּיךָ הַיָּמִים.
כֹּל יְמֵי חַיֶּיךָ הַלֵּילוֹת.

וַחֲכָמִים אוֹמְרִים

יְמֵי חַיֶּיךָ הָעוֹלָם הַזֶּה.
כֹּל יְמֵי חַיֶּיךָ לְהָבִיא לִימוֹת הַמָּשִׁיחַ:

Prison Labor

The Four Children

אַרְבָּעַת הַבָּנִים

Blessed is the Omnipresent, blessed is he. Blessed is He who gave the Torah to his nation Israel, Blessed is He.

בָּרוּךְ הַמָּקוֹם, בָּרוּךְ הוּא, בָּרוּךְ שֶׁנָּתַן תּוֹרָה לְעַמּוֹ יִשְׂרָאֵל, בָּרוּךְ הוּא.

The Torah speaks of four children:
The wise, the wicked, the simple, and the one who does not know how to ask.

כְּנֶגֶד אַרְבָּעָה בָנִים דִּבְּרָה תוֹרָה:
אֶחָד חָכָם, וְאֶחָד רָשָׁע, וְאֶחָד תָּם, וְאֶחָד שֶׁאֵינוֹ יוֹדֵעַ לִשְׁאוֹל.

What does the wise child say?
What are the laws and statutes and rules that God has commanded you? You must explain to him all the rules of Passover, including even the detail that we do not eat anything after the Passover offering, even the afikoman.

חָכָם מָה הוּא אוֹמֵר?
מָה הָעֵדוֹת וְהַחֻקִּים וְהַמִּשְׁפָּטִים אֲשֶׁר צִוָּה יי אֱלֹהֵינוּ אֶתְכֶם. וְאַף אַתָּה אֱמוֹר לוֹ כְּהִלְכוֹת הַפֶּסַח: אֵין מַפְטִירִין אַחַר הַפֶּסַח אֲפִיקוֹמָן:

The wicked child, what does he say?
What is the use of this ritual to you? To you and not to him! Because he has excluded himself from the community, he has transgressed a fundamental teaching of our faith. You must set his teeth on edge. Say to him: Because of this God did for me, when I went out of Egypt. For me and not for him. **If he had been there, he would not have been redeemed**.

רָשָׁע מָה הוּא אוֹמֵר?
מָה הָעֲבוֹדָה הַזֹּאת לָכֶם. לָכֶם - וְלֹא לוֹ. וּלְפִי שֶׁהוֹצִיא אֶת עַצְמוֹ מִן הַכְּלָל כָּפַר בְּעִקָּר. וְאַף אַתָּה הַקְהֵה אֶת שִׁנָּיו וֶאֱמוֹר לוֹ:
"בַּעֲבוּר זֶה עָשָׂה יי לִי בְּצֵאתִי מִמִּצְרָיִם". לִי וְלֹא לוֹ. **אִלּוּ הָיָה שָׁם, לֹא הָיָה נִגְאָל:**

What does the simple child say?
What is this? You must explain to him: With a strong hand God took us out from slavery in Egypt.

תָּם מָה הוּא אוֹמֵר?
מַה זֹּאת? וְאָמַרְתָּ אֵלָיו "בְּחוֹזֶק יָד הוֹצִיאָנוּ יי מִמִּצְרָיִם מִבֵּית עֲבָדִים".

The child who does not know how to ask,
you must make conversation with him. This is as it says, "Tell your son on that day: Because of this God did for me, when I went out of Egypt."

וְשֶׁאֵינוֹ יוֹדֵעַ לִשְׁאוֹל -
אַתְּ פְּתַח לוֹ, שֶׁנֶּאֱמַר, וְהִגַּדְתָּ לְבִנְךָ בַּיּוֹם הַהוּא לֵאמֹר, בַּעֲבוּר זֶה עָשָׂה יי לִי בְּצֵאתִי מִמִּצְרָיִם.

Slavery as Punishment

U.S. Constitution

The United States constitution still allows slavery to be used as punishment. Slavery was abolished in 1865 by the 13th amendment. But that amendment makes punishment an exception. It reads:

Neither slavery nor involuntary servitude, except as punishment for crime whereof the party shall have been duly convicted, shall exist within the United States.

Slavery for the Wicked?

The Haggadah says the wicked child would have been left as a slave in Egypt, implying that enslavement is a suitable punishment for the wicked.

If prisoners idly loaf about, imprisonment would hardly be a deterrent for crime. And since prisoners are provided food, clothing, and shelter, it makes sense that they should work to defray some of that cost.

Yet from the Soviet gulags to 19th century British prisoners forced to climb treadmills for hours to power mills and pumps, history is filled with examples of prisoners being cruelly abused and overworked. Here are some reasons prisoners should not be subjected to hard labor:

- Prisoners have almost no protection from physical or sexual abuse. Anyone punished by hard labor will likely be severely mistreated.

- There is no clear answer as to what crimes are severe enough to deserve hard labor as punishment. Society may therefore be tempted to incarcerate more citizens and work them at hard labor to perpetrate oppression or for economic gain.

- Prisoners performing hard labor become much like slaves. Slavery may be such an affront to human dignity it can never be justified.

The U.S. currently spends about $80 billion per year to hold 2.2 million people in prison. It makes sense they should work to pay some of that cost. But how do we protect prisoners from exploitation? And when prisoners work at vital, hard to fill jobs such as fighting forest fires does that create a disincentive to reform our criminal justice system?

Religious Freedom

Should we tell the story of the Exodus on the first day of the (Hebrew) month? No, because the Torah says **"on that day."** If we must tell the story on that day, perhaps then we should begin while it is still daylight? No, becase the Torah says, **"because of this."** Because of this means at the time when matzah and the bitter herbs are set before us.

In the beginning our ancestors worshipped idols, and now God has brought us near to serve him, as it says, "Joshua said to the nation: Thus says God, the Lord of Israel. Your ancestors always lived across the river, Terach the father of Abraham and Nachor, and they worshipped foreign gods. I took your father Abraham from across the river, and took him through the land of Cana'an. I gave him multiple offspring, and I gave him Isaac. I gave to Isaac Jacob and Esau. To Esau I gave Mt. Seir as an inheritance. Jacob and his sons went down to Egypt." (Joshua 24)

יָכוֹל מֵראשׁ חוֹדֶשׁ?

תַּלְמוּד לוֹמַר **בַּיוֹם הַהוּא.**

אִי בַּיוֹם הַהוּא יָכוֹל מִבְּעוֹד יוֹם?

תַּלְמוּד לוֹמַר **בַּעֲבוּר זֶה** -

בַּעֲבוּר זֶה לֹא אָמַרְתִּי,

אֶלָּא בְּשָׁעָה שֶׁיֵּשׁ

מַצָּה וּמָרוֹר מֻנָּחִים לְפָנֶיךָ.

מִתְּחִלָּה עוֹבְדֵי עֲבוֹדָה זָרָה הָיוּ אֲבוֹתֵינוּ, וְעַכְשָׁיו קֵרְבָנוּ הַמָּקוֹם לַעֲבֹדָתוֹ, שֶׁנֶּאֱמַר: "וַיֹּאמֶר יְהוֹשֻׁעַ אֶל כָּל הָעָם, כֹּה אָמַר יי אֱלֹהֵי יִשְׂרָאֵל: בְּעֵבֶר הַנָּהָר יָשְׁבוּ אֲבוֹתֵיכֶם מֵעוֹלָם, תֶּרַח אֲבִי אַבְרָהָם וַאֲבִי נָחוֹר, וַיַּעַבְדוּ אֱלֹהִים אֲחֵרִים. וָאֶקַּח אֶת אֲבִיכֶם אֶת אַבְרָהָם מֵעֵבֶר הַנָּהָר וָאוֹלֵךְ אוֹתוֹ בְּכָל אֶרֶץ כְּנָעַן, וָאַרְבֶּה אֶת זַרְעוֹ וָאֶתֶּן לוֹ אֶת יִצְחָק, וָאֶתֵּן לְיִצְחָק אֶת יַעֲקֹב וְאֶת עֵשָׂיו. וָאֶתֵּן לְעֵשָׂו אֶת הַר שֵׂעִיר לָרֶשֶׁת אֹתוֹ, וְיַעֲקֹב וּבָנָיו יָרְדוּ מִצְרָיִם."

Universal Declaration of Human Rights, Article 18

Everyone has the right to freedom of thought, conscience and religion; this right includes freedom to change his religion or belief, and freedom, either alone or in community with others and in public or private, to manifest his religion or belief in teaching, practice, worship and observance.

Hated, but Remains a Jew

How can one Jew hate another, for it says (Leviticus 19:16) 'do not hate your brother in your heart'? Our Rabbis explain this can be where one Jew saw another about to sin, warned him, but the sinner still did not change his ways. It is a mitzvah to hate such a person...

One who leaves the Jewish faith remains a Jew... even though he may sin he is still a part of Israel and he does not lose his status as part of the Jewish people.

– Maimonides Laws of Murder and Safeguarding Life 13:14 and Responsa Marriage 29

Judaism and Human Rights

While freedom to change one's religion is understood as a human right, Judaism does not recognize an ability to convert out (and often makes it difficult to convert in).

What should we do when Jewish laws or teachings do not seem compatible with human rights?

Reparations

Blessed is he who keeps his promise to Israel, blessed is he. For the Holy One, Blessed is He, calculated the time of our redemption, to fulfill the covenant with Abraham, as it says: God said to Abram, know that your descendants will be strangers in a foreign land, and they will be enslaved and oppressed for four hundred years. Then I will judge the nation that enslaved them, **and they will go out with great wealth.** (Genesis 15:13).

בָּרוּךְ שׁוֹמֵר הַבְטָחָתוֹ לְיִשְׂרָאֵל, בָּרוּךְ הוּא. שֶׁהַקָּדוֹשׁ בָּרוּךְ הוּא חִשַּׁב אֶת הַקֵּץ, לַעֲשׂוֹת כְּמוֹ שֶׁאָמַר לְאַבְרָהָם אָבִינוּ בִּבְרִית בֵּין הַבְּתָרִים, שֶׁנֶּאֱמַר: וַיֹּאמֶר לְאַבְרָם, יָדֹעַ תֵּדַע כִּי גֵר יִהְיֶה זַרְעֲךָ בְּאֶרֶץ לֹא לָהֶם, וַעֲבָדוּם וְעִנּוּ אֹתָם אַרְבַּע מֵאוֹת שנה. וְגַם אֶת הַגּוֹי אֲשֶׁר יַעֲבֹדוּ דָּן אָנֹכִי **וְאַחֲרֵי כֵן יֵצְאוּ, בִּרְכֻשׁ גָּדוֹל:**

Reparations in the Torah

When your Hebrew brother is sold to you as a slave for six years, in the seventh year you shall set him free. And when you set him free, he shall not go empty handed. Give him from your flocks, your threshing, and your winepress..."
– Devarim 15:13.

"Since he has nothing...how will he support himself if he is not given these gifts?"
– Commentary on the Torah by Rabbi Hezekiah ben Manoah (Chizkuni) 13th century.

According to United Nations resolutions and the Rome Statute, human rights abusers must pay their victims compensation. This is for two reasons:

1. **Practical** – To enable the victims to begin new lives.

2. **Moral** – For the abuser to take responsibility for the injustice, they must attempt to repair the harm they've done.

Reparations include:

Restitution:
Restitutions are payments designed to restore the victim to the situation they were in before the abuse occurred. This may mean restoring the person's place of residence, returning their property, or restoring their citizenship.

Compensation:
This is to make up for the harm done, and can include making up for lost opportunities for employment or education.

Rehabilitation:
This consists of medical or psychological care.

Satisfaction:
This includes such things as public apology and accepting responsibility by the group that caused the abuse.

Commemoration and memorials to the victims:
This includes verification of the facts of what happened and public disclosure of the truth, search for those who may have disappeared, and proper burial of victims.

Guarantees of non-repetition:
These are political, legal, or educational changes designed to prevent the violations from recurring

Problems with Reparations

It only seems fair that victims of human rights abuses should receive reparations, just like victims of other crimes are entitled to compensation. Survivors of genocide, slavery, and war crimes may have lost everything and depend on reparations to rebuild their lives.

Israeli Prime Minister David Ben Gurion demanded reparations from Germany after the Holocaust, so that "the murderers do not also become the heirs". But many objected, saying that accepting money would lighten the Germans' guilt. Another problem with reparations is it often takes a long time to arrange for them to be paid. By then it can be difficult to determine who are the actual victims or their heirs, and those paying may no longer be the ones who committed the crimes. This is a major objection to paying reparations for slavery in the United States.

When do reparations help rectify injustice?
When do they create a new injustice, or lighten the conscience of those who have committed crimes?

Menachem Begin, head of the Herut party, protesting against accepting Holocaust reparations from Germany in March 1952 in Tel Aviv.

The sign reads:
"Our honor shall not be sold for money; Our blood shall not be atoned by goods. We shall wipe out the disgrace!"

From the National Photo Collection of Israel

AGREEMENT BETWEEN THE STATE OF ISRAEL
AND THE FEDERAL REPUBLIC OF GERMANY

Signed on 10 September 1952, at Luxembourg

*Came into force upon the exchange of the Instruments of Ratification on
27 March, 1953, at United Nations Headquarters, New York.*

WHEREAS unspeakable criminal acts were perpetrated against the Jewish people
during the National-Socialist régime of terror
AND WHEREAS by a declaration in the Bundestag on 27th September, 1951,
the Government of the Federal Republic of Germany made known their determin-
ation, within the limits of their capacity, to make good the material damage
caused by these acts
AND WHEREAS the State of Israel has assumed the heavy burden of resettling
so great a number of uprooted and destitute Jewish refugees from Germany and
from territories formerly under German rule and has on this basis advanced a
claim against the Federal Republic of Germany for global recompense for the
cost of the integration of these refugees
NOW THEREFORE the State of Israel and the Federal Republic of Germany
have agreed as follows:—

ARTICLE 1

(a) The Federal Republic of Germany shall, in view of the considerations herein-
before recited, pay to the State of Israel the sum of 3,000 million Deutsche
Mark.

(b) In addition, the Federal Republic of Germany shall, in compliance with the
obligations undertaken in Article 1 of Protocol No. 2 this day drawn up and
signed between Germany and the

Train set manufactured by Maschinenfabrik Esslingen in the old Jerusalem Railway Station, shortly after delivery as part of the reparations agreement with Germany, 1956.

Genocide

He has stood up for our ancestors and for us. Because not just once have **enemies risen up to destroy us.** Rather in every generation they rise up to destroy us, and the Holy One, Blessed is He, saves us from them.

Go and learn what Lavan the Aramean attempted to do to our patriarch Jacob. Pharoah only decreed against the baby boys, but Lavan **attempted to destroy all,** as it says: A wandering Aramean was my father, and he went down with small numbers to Egypt to live there. And he became there a great nation, powerful and numerous.

וְהִיא שֶׁעָמְדָה לַאֲבוֹתֵינוּ וְלָנוּ. שֶׁלֹּא אֶחָד בִּלְבָד **עָמַד עָלֵינוּ לְכַלוֹתֵנוּ,** אֶלָּא שֶׁבְּכָל דּוֹר וָדוֹר עוֹמְדִים עָלֵינוּ לְכַלוֹתֵנוּ, וְהַקָּדוֹשׁ בָּרוּךְ הוּא מַצִּילֵנוּ מִיָּדָם.

צֵא וּלְמַד מַה בִּקֵּשׁ לָבָן הָאֲרַמִּי לַעֲשׂוֹת לְיַעֲקֹב אָבִינוּ: שֶׁפַּרְעֹה לֹא גָזַר אֶלָּא עַל הַזְּכָרִים, **וְלָבָן בִּקֵּשׁ לַעֲקֹר אֶת־הַכֹּל.** שֶׁנֶּאֱמַר: אֲרַמִּי אֹבֵד אָבִי, וַיֵּרֶד מִצְרַיְמָה וַיָּגָר שָׁם בִּמְתֵי מְעָט, וַיְהִי שָׁם לְגוֹי גָּדוֹל, עָצוּם וָרָב.

The Term Genocide

The term genocide was coined in 1944 from the Greek prefix genos, which means race or tribe, and the Latin suffix cide, which means killing. Just like homicide is the killing of one person, genocide is the killing of an entire group. The Rome Statute defines genocide as harm committed with intent to destroy, in whole or in part, a national, ethnic, racial or religious group.

Killing One Person is Like Killing the World

The Rabbis warn against speaking out only about large scale atrocities such as genocide by saying: "Man was created alone to teach that whoever kills one person is as if he has destroyed the entire world, and whoever saves one life it as though he has saved the entire world."

–Talmud Sanhedrin 37a

The Significance of Genocide

"Every year politicians repeat 'never again,' and now, we see that these words simply mean nothing. A people is being destroyed in Europe," Ukraine President Volodymyr Zelensky said to the German Parliament in March 2022, complaining that countries put their own political and military considerations above moral commitments in refusing to aid his country.

Source: https://www.timesofisrael.com/zelensky-tells-german-mps-never-again-holocaust-slogan-is-now-meaningless/

As Jews, from Pharoah to Haman to Hitler we are all too familiar with genocide. But as violence against innocent people continues all around the world, what lessons have we learned? What does it mean to say 'Never again?'

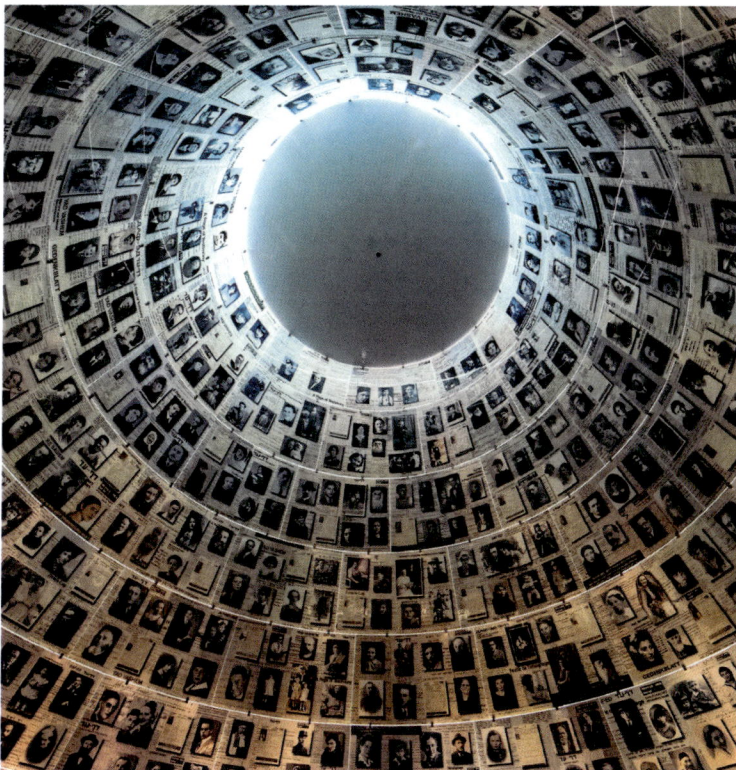

Hall of Names in the Yad Vashem Holocaust Memorial, Jerusalem

Refugees

He went down to Egypt, forced to go according to the Torah.
He lived there – this teaches that Jacob only went to dwell temporarily in Egypt, not to live there permanently. This is as it is written in the Torah: They said to Pharoah: We have come to live in the land, since there is nothing for your servants' sheep to graze on, for the famine is very severe in the land of Cana'an. Now please let your servants settle in the land of Goshen.

וַיֵּרֶד מִצְרַיְמָה – אָנוּס עַל פִּי הַדִּבּוּר.

וַיָּגָר שָׁם. מְלַמֵּד שֶׁלֹּא יָרַד יַעֲקֹב אָבִינוּ לְהִשְׁתַּקֵּעַ בְּמִצְרַיִם אֶלָּא לָגוּר שָׁם, שֶׁנֶּאֱמַר: וַיֹּאמְרוּ אֶל-פַּרְעֹה, לָגוּר בָּאָרֶץ בָּאנוּ, כִּי אֵין מִרְעֶה לַצֹּאן אֲשֶׁר לַעֲבָדֶיךָ, כִּי כָבֵד הָרָעָב בְּאֶרֶץ כְּנָעַן. וְעַתָּה יֵשְׁבוּ-נָא עֲבָדֶיךָ בְּאֶרֶץ גֹּשֶׁן.

From the 1951 Refugee Convention

"A refugee is someone who is unable or unwilling to return to their country of origin owing to a well-founded fear of being persecuted for reasons of race, religion, nationality, membership of a particular social group, or political opinion."

Countries are obligated to shelter refugees. Someone who chooses to move in search of better economic opportunities is a migrant. Countries do not have to accept migrants and can force them to return home.

Roles Reverse

Whoever shows mercy towards the poor, God has mercy upon him. Note: A person should take to heart that at every moment he requests his own sustenance from God. Just as he wants God to hear his cries, so he should hear the cries of the poor. He should also take to heart that situations are always changing, and in the end he, his children, or his grandchildren may also wind up poor. Whoever has mercy upon others, others will have mercy upon him.

– Shulchan Aruch Laws of Tzedakah 247:3

Was Jacob a migrant or a refugee?

Jacob and his family went to Egypt to escape famine in Canaan. This would seem to be a compelling reason to receive help – if Jacob had been sent back to Canaan, he would have faced starvation and possible death!

But famine, natural disasters, gang violence, and warfare are not included in the refugee convention as entitling people to international protection, and countries cannot afford to take in the enormous numbers of people who may flee such things.

Was Egypt required to accept Jacob's family? What should be done when whole populations flee violence or natural disasters looking for new places to settle?

Reproductive Rights

With small numbers, as it says in the Torah: As a family of 70 your ancestors went down to Egypt. **And now, God has made you numerous as the stars of the heavens.**

And there you became a nation: This teaches that Israel remained distinct. Large and numerous, as it says in the Torah: **And the children of Israel were fruitful and multiplied,** they became very strong and numerous, **and the land was filled with them.**

Great, mighty, as it is written. "The children of Israel were fruitful and increased greatly; they multiplied and became mighty, and the land was full of them." And numerous, as it is written: "I made you as populous as the plants of the field; you grew up and wore choice adornments; your breasts were firm and your hair grew long; yet, you were bare and naked."

בִּמְתֵי מְעָט. כְּמָה שֶׁנֶּאֱמַר: בְּשִׁבְעִים נֶפֶשׁ יָרְדוּ אֲבוֹתֶיךָ מִצְרָיְמָה, **וְעַתָּה שָׂמְךָ ה' אֱלֹהֶיךָ כְּכוֹכְבֵי הַשָּׁמַיִם לָרֹב.**

וַיְהִי שָׁם לְגוֹי. מְלַמֵּד שֶׁהָיוּ יִשְׂרָאֵל מְצֻיָּנִים שָׁם. גָּדוֹל עָצוּם – כְּמָה שֶׁנֶּאֱמַר: **וּבְנֵי יִשְׂרָאֵל פָּרוּ וַיִּשְׁרְצוּ וַיִּרְבּוּ וַיַּעַצְמוּ בִּמְאֹד מְאֹד, וַתִּמָּלֵא הָאָרֶץ אֹתָם.**

וָרָב. כְּמָה שֶׁנֶּאֱמַר: רְבָבָה כְּצֶמַח הַשָּׂדֶה נְתַתִּיךְ, וַתִּרְבִּי וַתִּגְדְּלִי וַתָּבֹאִי בַּעֲדִי עֲדָיִים, שָׁדַיִם נָכֹנוּ וּשְׂעָרֵךְ צִמֵּחַ, וְאַתְּ עֵרֹם וְעֶרְיָה. וָאֶעֱבֹר עָלַיִךְ וָאֶרְאֵךְ מִתְבּוֹסֶסֶת בְּדָמָיִךְ, וָאֹמַר לָךְ בְּדָמַיִךְ חֲיִי, וָאֹמַר לָךְ בְּדָמַיִךְ חֲיִי.

Universal Declaration of Human Rights, Article 16

Men and women of full age, without any limitation due to race, nationality or religion, have the right to marry and to found a family.

Population Growth and Reproductive Rights

While human population remained relatively stable for many thousands of years, in the last century it has increased rapidly. This may lead to environmental and economic pressures.

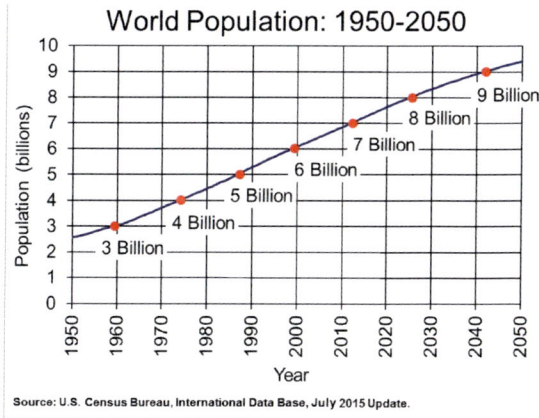

World Population: 1950-2050

3 Billion
4 Billion
5 Billion
6 Billion
7 Billion
8 Billion
9 Billion

Source: U.S. Census Bureau, International Data Base, July 2015 Update.

Be Fruitful and Multiply

God blessed them (Adam and Eve) and said to them, 'Be fruitful and multiply, fill up the land and conquer it.

Even if a man has already fulfilled the mitzvah of 'be fruitful and multiply' he is still commanded by the Rabbis to have more children as long as he is able.

– Genesis 1:28 and Maimonides Laws of Marriage 15:16.

Who Decides How Many Children?

Should governments be able to limit how many children we can have in order to preserve natural or economic resources, or is having children a personal matter that no government should interfere with?

Workers' Rights

The Egyptians suspected us of evil and afflicted us; **they imposed hard labor upon us.**

The Egyptians suspected us of evil, as it is written: "Let us deal with them wisely lest they multiply, and, if we happen to be at war, they may join our enemies and fight against us and then leave the country."

And afflicted us, as it is written: "They set taskmasters over them in order to oppress them with their burdens; the people of Israel built Pithom and Raamses as storecities for Pharaoh."

They imposed hard labor upon us, as it is written: **"They imposed back-breaking labor upon the people of Israel."**

וַיָּרֵעוּ אֹתָנוּ הַמִּצְרִים וַיְעַנּוּנוּ.

וַיִּתְּנוּ עָלֵינוּ עֲבֹדָה קָשָׁה.

וַיָּרֵעוּ אֹתָנוּ הַמִּצְרִים. כְּמָה שֶׁנֶּאֱמַר:

הָבָה נִתְחַכְּמָה לוֹ. פֶּן־יִרְבֶּה, וְהָיָה

כִּי־תִקְרֶאנָה מִלְחָמָה, וְנוֹסַף גַּם

הוּא עַל־שֹׂנְאֵינוּ, וְנִלְחַם־בָּנוּ וְעָלָה

מִן־הָאָרֶץ:

וַיְעַנּוּנוּ. כְּמָה שֶׁנֶּאֱמַר: וַיָּשִׂימוּ עָלָיו

שָׂרֵי מִסִּים, לְמַעַן עַנֹּתוֹ בְּסִבְלֹתָם:

וַיִּבֶן עָרֵי מִסְכְּנוֹת לְפַרְעֹה, אֶת־פִּתֹם

וְאֶת־רַעַמְסֵס:

וַיִּתְּנוּ עָלֵינוּ עֲבֹדָה קָשָׁה. כְּמָה שֶׁנֶּאֱמַר:

וַיַּעֲבִדוּ מִצְרַיִם אֶת־בְּנֵי יִשְׂרָאֵל בְּפָרֶךְ:

All According to Local Custom

If one hires workers and tells them to start early or stay late, in a place where it is not customary for workers to do so they cannot be compelled. In a place where the custom is to provide workers with food, employers must do so. If the custom is to also provide sweets, the employer must do so as well. All is according to local custom.

– Mishna Baba Metzia 7:1

From the International Labor Organization Constitution (adopted in 1919)

Whereas universal and lasting peace can be established only if it is based upon social justice;

And whereas conditions of labour exist involving such injustice, hardship and privation to large numbers of people as to produce unrest so great that the peace and harmony of the world are imperilled; and an improvement of those conditions is urgently required;

Whereas also the failure of any nation to adopt humane conditions of labour is an obstacle in the way of other nations which desire to improve the conditions in their own countries;

The High Contracting Parties, moved by sentiments of justice and humanity as well as by the desire to secure the permanent peace of the world, and with a view to attaining the objectives set forth in this Preamble, agree to the following Constitution of the International Labour Organization.

Must all Workers Have the Same Rights?

Many products we purchase are manufactured in far away places where costs are lower. This is often due to less safe working conditions and low pay. Are countries entitled to set lower standards of workers' rights if they believe that is in their development interests? Or are all workers entitled to equivalent pay and conditions no matter where they live, such that it is wrong for a company to shift manufacturing to countries where they can pay employees less and have them work in inferior conditions?

Sexual Exploitation

We cried out to God, God of our fathers, and God heard our voice, saw our suffering, our labor, and our distress (Deut. 26:7).

וַנִּצְעַק אֶל יְיָ אֱלֹהֵי אֲבֹתֵינוּ, וַיִּשְׁמַע יְיָ אֶת קֹלֵנוּ, וַיַּרְא אֶת עָנְיֵנוּ וְאֶת עֲמָלֵנוּ וְאֶת לַחֲצֵנוּ.

We cried out to God, God of our fathers: As it says in the Torah: During those many days, the King of Egypt died. The children of Israel groaned from the labor and cried out. Their pleas rose up to God from their work (Exodus 2:23).

וַנִּצְעַק אֶל יְיָ אֱלֹהֵי אֲבֹתֵינוּ - כְּמָה שֶׁנֶּאֱמַר: וַיְהִי בַיָּמִים הָרַבִּים הָהֵם וַיָּמָת מֶלֶךְ מִצְרַיִם, וַיֵּאָנְחוּ בְנֵי יִשְׂרָאֵל מִן הָעֲבוֹדָה וַיִּזְעָקוּ, וַתַּעַל שַׁוְעָתָם אֶל הָאֱלֹהִים מִן הָעֲבֹדָה.

God heard our cries: as it says: God heard their groans, and God remembered his covenant, Abraham, Isaac, and Jacob (Exodus 2:24).

וַיִּשְׁמַע יְיָ אֶת קֹלֵנוּ - כְּמָה שֶׁנֶּאֱמַר: וַיִּשְׁמַע אֱלֹהִים אֶת נַאֲקָתָם, וַיִּזְכֹּר אֱלֹהִים אֶת בְּרִיתוֹ אֶת אַבְרָהָם, אֶת יִצְחָק וְאֶת יַעֲקֹב.

God saw our suffering: This is the stoppage of relations between husbands and wives, as it says in the Torah: God saw the children of Israel, and God knew (Exodus 2:25).

וַיַּרְא אֶת עָנְיֵנוּ - זוֹ פְּרִישׁוּת דֶּרֶךְ אֶרֶץ, כְּמָה שֶׁנֶּאֱמַר: וַיַּרְא אֱלֹהִים אֶת בְּנֵי יִשְׂרָאֵל וַיֵּדַע אֱלֹהִים.

And our labor: These are our lost sons. As it says in the Torah: All baby boys that are born shall be thrown into the river, but the girls shall live (Exodus 1:22).

וְאֶת עֲמָלֵנוּ - אֵלּוּ הַבָּנִים. כְּמָה שֶׁנֶּאֱמַר: כָּל הַבֵּן הַיִּלּוֹד הַיְאֹרָה תַּשְׁלִיכֻהוּ וְכָל הַבַּת תְּחַיּוּן.

And our oppression: This is the urgency with which they were worked. As it says, "And I saw the oppression with which Egypt was pressuring them." (Shmot 3:9)

וְאֶת לַחֲצֵנוּ - זֶה הַדְּחַק, כְּמָה שֶׁנֶּאֱמַר: וְגַם רָאִיתִי אֶת הַלַּחַץ אֲשֶׁר מִצְרַיִם לֹחֲצִים אֹתָם.

Sexual Exploitation in Egypt

For what reason did Pharaoh spare the baby girls? He said, let us kill the boys, then when the girls grow up we can take them for ourselves. He did this because the Egyptians were awash in sexual immorality
– Midrash Rabbah on Exodus 1:22

Sex Work and Trafficking

Preamble to New Zealand Prostitution Reform Act of 2003

The purpose of this Act is to decriminalise prostitution (while not endorsing or morally sanctioning prostitution or its use) and to create a framework that;

- safeguards the human rights of sex workers and protects them from exploitation;

- promotes the welfare and occupational health and safety of sex workers;

- is conducive to public health;

- prohibits the use in prostitution of persons under 18 years of age.

This act goes on to make sex work legal in New Zealand

Preamble to Canadian Protection of Communities and Exploited Persons Act of 2014

- Whereas the Parliament of Canada has grave concerns about the exploitation that is inherent in prostitution and the risks of violence posed to those who engage in it;

- Whereas the Parliament of Canada recognizes the social harm caused by the objectification of the human body and the commodification of sexual activity;

- Whereas it is important to protect human dignity and the equality of all Canadians by discouraging prostitution, which has a disproportionate impact on women and children;

- Whereas the Parliament of Canada wishes to encourage those who engage in prostitution to report incidents of violence and to leave prostitution;

This act makes it illegal to pay for sex work in Canada

Sex Work and the Law

Some view sex work as inherently degrading, and closely associated with trafficking and violence. In this view sex work itself is a violation of human rights. Others believe that while no one should be coerced or trafficked, choosing sex work voluntarily is an exercise of personal autonomy and freedom. In this view criminalization itself is what causes many of the industry's problems. When sex work is legal, workers can freely report abuses to authorities and seek health care without fear of legal repercussions, and cooperate with police to report trafficking or violence.

Is criminalizing sex work necessary to fight trafficking and safeguard the rights of the sex workers themselves? Or is criminalization an affront to the human rights of sex workers and not necessary or even counterproductive in the battle against trafficking?

And God took us out of Egypt with a strong hand, an outstretched arm, great awe, signs, and wonders (Devarim 26:8).

'God took us out of Egypt': Not via an angel, not via a seraph, not via a messenger. Rather the holy one, blessed be he, himself in his glory. As it says: 'I will pass through the land of Egypt on that night, and strike every first born in Egypt, from man to animal, and against all of Egypt's Gods I will bring judgment, for I am the Lord.' (Exodus 12:12).

'I will pass through the land of Egypt'- I and not an angel.

'I will strike every first born in Egypt'- I and not a seraph.

'Against all of Egypt's Gods I will bring judgment'-

וַיּוֹצִאֵנוּ יְיָ מִמִּצְרַיִם בְּיָד חֲזָקָה וּבִזְרֹעַ נְטוּיָה, וּבְמֹרָא גָּדֹל, וּבְאֹתוֹת וּבְמֹפְתִים.

וַיּוֹצִאֵנוּ יְיָ מִמִּצְרַיִם - לֹא עַל יְדֵי מַלְאָךְ, וְלֹא עַל יְדֵי שָׂרָף, וְלֹא עַל יְדֵי שָׁלִיחַ, אֶלָּא הַקָּדוֹשׁ בָּרוּךְ הוּא בִּכְבוֹדוֹ וּבְעַצְמוֹ, שֶׁנֶּאֱמַר: וְעָבַרְתִּי בְאֶרֶץ מִצְרַיִם בַּלַּיְלָה הַזֶּה, וְהִכֵּיתִי כָל בְּכוֹר בְּאֶרֶץ מִצְרַיִם מֵאָדָם וְעַד בְּהֵמָה, וּבְכָל אֱלֹהֵי מִצְרַיִם אֶעֱשֶׂה שְׁפָטִים. אֲנִי יְיָ.

וְעָבַרְתִּי בְאֶרֶץ מִצְרַיִם בַּלַּיְלָה הַזֶּה - אֲנִי וְלֹא מַלְאָךְ.

וְהִכֵּיתִי כָל בְּכוֹר בְּאֶרֶץ מִצְרַיִם - אֲנִי וְלֹא שָׂרָף.

וּבְכָל אֱלֹהֵי מִצְרַיִם אֶעֱשֶׂה שְׁפָטִים -

44

I and not a messenger.

'I am the Lord'-

I am the Lord and no other.

'With a strong hand'-

This is the animal disease, as it says, 'Behold, the hand of God is set against your flocks that are in the field, against the horses and donkeys and camels, the cattle and sheep, a very heavy plague.' (Exodus 9:13).

'With an outstretched arm'-

This is the sword, as it says, 'His sword is drawn in his hand, outstretched against Jerusalem.' (I Chronicles 21:16).

'With great awe'-

This refers to the revelation of the divine presence. As it says, 'Has any God attempted to come and take for himself one nation from the midst of another, with trials, signs, wonders, and warfare?

'With signs'-

This is the staff, as it says, 'And this staff you shall take in your hand, to do with it the signs.' (Exodus 4:17).

'With wonders'-

This is the blood. As it says, "I will place signs against the heaven and the earth.'

Blood. Fire. Pillars of Smoke

Another interpretation:

'With a strong hand'- 2 plagues.

'An outstretched arm'- 2 plagues.

'Great awe'- 2 plagues.

'Signs'- 2 plagues.

'And with wonders'- 2 plagues.

אֲנִי וְלֹא הַשָּׁלִיחַ.

אֲנִי יְיָ -

אֲנִי הוּא וְלֹא אַחֵר.

בְּיָד חֲזָקָה -

זוֹ הַדֶּבֶר, כְּמָה שֶׁנֶּאֱמַר: הִנֵּה יַד יְיָ הוֹיָה בְּמִקְנְךָ אֲשֶׁר בַּשָּׂדֶה, בַּסּוּסִים, בַּחֲמֹרִים, בַּגְּמַלִּים, בַּבָּקָר וּבַצֹּאן, דֶּבֶר כָּבֵד מְאֹד.

וּבִזְרֹעַ נְטוּיָה -

זוֹ הַחֶרֶב, כְּמָה שֶׁנֶּאֱמַר: וְחַרְבּוֹ שְׁלוּפָה בְּיָדוֹ, נְטוּיָה עַל יְרוּשָׁלָיִם.

וּבְמֹרָא גָּדֹל -

זוֹ גִלּוּי שְׁכִינָה, כְּמָה שֶׁנֶּאֱמַר: אוֹ הֲנִסָּה אֱלֹהִים לָבֹא לָקַחַת לוֹ גוֹי מִקֶּרֶב גּוֹי בְּמַסֹּת בְּאֹתֹת וּבְמוֹפְתִים, וּבְמִלְחָמָה וּבְיָד חֲזָקָה וּבִזְרֹעַ נְטוּיָה, וּבְמוֹרָאִים גְּדֹלִים, כְּכֹל אֲשֶׁר עָשָׂה לָכֶם יְיָ אֱלֹהֵיכֶם בְּמִצְרַיִם לְעֵינֶיךָ.

וּבְאֹתוֹת -

זֶה הַמַּטֶּה, כְּמָה שֶׁנֶּאֱמַר: וְאֶת הַמַּטֶּה הַזֶּה תִּקַּח בְּיָדֶךָ, אֲשֶׁר תַּעֲשֶׂה בּוֹ אֶת הָאֹתֹת.

וּבְמוֹפְתִים -

זֶה הַדָּם. כְּמָה שֶׁנֶּאֱמַר: וְנָתַתִּי מוֹפְתִים, בַּשָּׁמַיִם וּבָאָרֶץ.

דָּם. וָאֵשׁ. וְתִימְרוֹת עָשָׁן.

דָּבָר אַחֵר:

בְּיָד חֲזָקָה - שְׁתַּיִם,

וּבִזְרֹעַ נְטוּיָה - שְׁתַּיִם,

וּבְמֹרָא גָּדֹל - שְׁתַּיִם,

בְּאֹתוֹת - שְׁתַּיִם,

וּבְמֹפְתִים - שְׁתַּיִם.

War Crimes - The Ten Plagues

We spill a drop of wine from our glass as we recite the
three signs and then the ten plagues.

There were 10 plagues that the Holy One,
blessed be he, brought upon Egypt, and
this is what they were:

אֵלּוּ עֶשֶׂר מַכּוֹת שֶׁהֵבִיא הַקָּדוֹשׁ בָּרוּךְ

הוּא עַל הַמִּצְרִים בְּמִצְרַיִם, וְאֵלּוּ הֵן:

Blood   דָּם

Frogs   צְפַרְדֵּעַ

Lice   כִּנִּים

Wild Beasts   עָרוֹב

Cattle Disease   דֶּבֶר

Boils   שְׁחִין

Hail   בָּרד

Locust   אַרְבֶּה

Darkness   חֹשֶׁךְ

Death of the First Born   מַכַּת בְּכוֹרוֹת

Rabbi Judah abbreviated the ten plagues
by composing three words from their Hebrew initials:

רַבִּי יְהוּדָה הָיָה
נוֹתֵן בָּהֶם סִמָּנִים:

D'tzach, Adash, B'achab   דְּצַ"ךְ עַד"שׁ בְּאַחַ"ב.

What are War Crimes?

War crimes are based on distinguishing between civilians and combatants. According to the Geneva Conventions, in war it is permitted to attack an enemy's military, but forbidden to target an enemy's civilians. A military must also take precautions to avoid harming civilians, and may not attack even a military target if doing so will cause civilian harm disproportionate to the military value of the attack.

War Crimes and the Ten Plagues?

It would certainly have been justified for the Israelites to attack Pharoah himself, along with the taskmasters and soldiers enforcing their bondage. But the plagues were indiscriminate, purposefully targeting the entire Egyptian population with the goal of inflicting widespread suffering.

Would the ten plagues have been forbidden by the Geneva Convention, and therefore today be considered war crimes? Was there a better way?

The destruction of Dresden, Germany
Beginning on the night of February 13, 1945, more than 1,200 British and then American heavy bombers dropped nearly 4,000 tons of high-explosive and incendiary bombs on Dresden in four successive raids. Casualty estimates range from 35,000 to 135,000. The city was damaged so badly that after the war nearly everything had to be demolished.
Credit: rarehistoricalphotos.com

47

Targeting Civilians Is Always Prohibited

Fighting Against Occupation and Domination

The Israelites might have argued that what the Egyptians were doing to them was so bad they should be able to target all of Egypt with the plagues if that's what was needed to go free. After all, the Israelites had been enslaved and their baby boys were being drowned in the Nile!

This rationale for targeting civilians is ruled out by a 1977 Protocol to the Geneva Convention. It specifically includes 'armed conflicts in which people are fighting against colonial domination and alien occupation' as circumstances in which all civilian protections still apply.

An Israeli policeman in Ashkelon storing rockets fired from Gaza. These rockets were fired indiscriminately at Israeli population centers, with no regard to avoiding civilian harm.

Who is a Civilian?

The Rabbis' Explanation

Our Rabbis were also troubled by the indiscriminate nature of the plagues. Rashi (a famous rabbinic commentator who lived in 11th century France) tried to justify this by writing that all of Egypt's first born were included in the final plague because all the Egyptians were guilty of celebrating Israel's enslavement.

– Rashi Exodus 12:29

Still Civilians

The Geneva Conventions define a civilian as anyone who is not a member of the military and not taking part in combat. Even people who do these three things retain their civilian status and may not be attacked:

Pay taxes or buy bonds that support the enemy's military.

Vote for or campaign on behalf of the enemy's leader.

Publicly state or believe that an enemy's crimes or atrocities are acceptable.

Propaganda for War

Rabbi Yossi the Galilean said: How do we know that since the Egyptians were struck by ten plagues in Egypt, by the sea they were struck by fifty?

In Egypt it says, 'The magicians said to Pharoah: It is the finger of God. (Exodus 8:16). By the sea what does it say? 'Israel saw the great hand that God had brought against Egypt, and the nation feared God. They believed in God and his servant Moses (Exodus 14:31).' They were struck by ten plagues from God's finger, so from this we conclude that in Egypt they were struck by ten plagues, but by the sea they were struck with fifty.

Rabbi Eliezer says: How do we know that every plague that the Holy One, blessed be he, brought against the Egyptians in Egypt consisted of four plagues?

It says, 'He will send against them his blazing anger, indignation, fury, woe, and delegation of destructive angels.' (Psalms 78:49).

'Indignation'- one. **'Fury'-** two. **'Woe'-** three

'Delegation of destructive angels'- four.

From this we conclude, in Egypt they were struck with forty plagues, and on the sea they were struck with two hundred.

Rabbi Akiva says: How do we know that every plague which the Holy One, blessed is he, brought upon the Egyptians in Egypt consisted of five plagues?

As it says, 'He will send against them his blazing anger, indignation, fury, woe, and delegation of destructive angels.' (Psalms 78:49).

'blazing anger'- one. **'Indignation'-** two.

'Fury'- three. **'Woe'-** four.

'Delegation of destructive angels'- five.

We conclude from this, in Egypt the Egyptians were struck by fifty plagues, and on the sea they were struck by two hundred fifty.

רַבִּי יוֹסֵי הַגְּלִילִי אוֹמֵר: מִנַּיִן אַתָּה אוֹמֵר שֶׁלָּקוּ הַמִּצְרִים בְּמִצְרַיִם עֶשֶׂר מַכּוֹת וְעַל הַיָּם לָקוּ חֲמִשִּׁים מַכּוֹת? בְּמִצְרַיִם מַה הוּא אוֹמֵר? וַיֹּאמְרוּ הַחַרְטֻמִּם אֶל פַּרְעֹה: אֶצְבַּע אֱלֹהִים הוּא. וְעַל הַיָּם מה הוּא אוֹמֵר? וַיַּרְא יִשְׂרָאֵל אֶת הַיָּד הַגְּדֹלָה אֲשֶׁר עָשָׂה ה' בְּמִצְרַיִם, וַיִּירְאוּ הָעָם אֶת ה', וַיַּאֲמִינוּ בַּיי וּבְמשֶׁה עַבְדּוֹ. כַּמָּה לָקוּ בְאֶצְבַּע? עֶשֶׂר מַכּוֹת. אֱמוֹר מֵעַתָּה: בְּמִצְרַיִם לָקוּ עֶשֶׂר מַכּוֹת וְעַל הַיָּם לָקוּ חֲמִשִּׁים מַכּוֹת.

רַבִּי אֱלִיעֶזֶר אוֹמֵר: מִנַּיִן שֶׁכָּל מַכָּה וּמַכָּה שֶׁהֵבִיא הַקָּדוֹשׁ בָּרוּךְ הוּא עַל הַמִּצְרִים בְּמִצְרַיִם הָיְתָה שֶׁל אַרְבַּע מַכּוֹת? שֶׁנֶּאֱמַר: יְשַׁלַּח בָּם חֲרוֹן אַפּוֹ, עֶבְרָה וָזַעַם וְצָרָה, מִשְׁלַחַת מַלְאֲכֵי רָעִים.

עֶבְרָה - אַחַת,

וָזַעַם - שְׁתַּיִם,

וְצָרָה - שָׁלֹשׁ,

מִשְׁלַחַת מַלְאֲכֵי רָעִים - אַרְבַּע.

אֱמוֹר מֵעַתָּה: בְּמִצְרַיִם לָקוּ אַרְבָּעִים מַכּוֹת וְעַל הַיָּם לָקוּ מָאתַיִם מַכּוֹת.

רַבִּי עֲקִיבָא אוֹמֵר: מִנַּיִן שֶׁכָּל מַכָּה וּמַכָּה שֶׁהֵבִיא הַקָּדוֹשׁ בָּרוּךְ הוּא עַל הַמִּצְרִים בְּמִצְרַיִם הָיְתָה שֶׁל חָמֵשׁ מַכּוֹת? שֶׁנֶּאֱמַר: יְשַׁלַּח בָּם חֲרוֹן אַפּוֹ, עֶבְרָה וָזַעַם וְצָרָה, מִשְׁלַחַת מַלְאֲכֵי רָעִים.

חֲרוֹן אַפּוֹ - אַחַת,

עֶבְרָה - שְׁתַּיִם,

וָזַעַם - שָׁלוֹשׁ,

וְצָרָה - אַרְבַּע,

מִשְׁלַחַת מַלְאֲכֵי רָעִים - חָמֵשׁ.

אֱמוֹר מֵעַתָּה: בְּמִצְרַיִם לָקוּ חֲמִשִּׁים מַכּוֹת וְעַל הַיָּם לָקוּ חֲמִשִּׁים וּמָאתַיִם מַכּוֹת.

Rejoice While Egyptians Are Drowning?

At that time when the Egyptians were drowning in the Red Sea the angels wanted to sing praises to God. The Holy One, blessed be he, replied: My handiwork is drowning, but you wish to sing?

– Talmud Sanhedrin 39b

From the International Covenant on Civil and Political Rights

Any propaganda for war shall be prohibited by law. Any advocacy of national, racial or religious hatred that constitutes incitement to discrimination, hostility or violence shall be prohibited by law.

Source: ICCPR Article 20

When Does it Become Propaganda?

It's only natural to want to see our oppressors suffer, and for a newly liberated people to celebrate its redemption. But when does this reach a point of demonizing and dehumanizing our enemies, thereby encouraging an endless cycle of war?

Dayeinu _____ דַּיֵּנוּ

How grateful must we be for all God has done for us!

כַּמָּה מַעֲלוֹת טוֹבוֹת לַמָּקוֹם עָלֵינוּ.

If he took us out of Egypt		
But did not bring judgement against them	- Dayeinu!	דַּיֵּנוּ.

אִלּוּ הוֹצִיאָנוּ מִמִּצְרַיִם

וְלֹא עָשָׂה בָהֶם שְׁפָטִים,

| If he brought judgment against them | | |
| But did not act against their Gods | -Dayeinu! | דַּיֵּנוּ. |

אִלּוּ עָשָׂה בָהֶם שְׁפָטִים,

ולא עָשָׂה בֵאלֹהֵיהֶם,

| If he acted against their Gods | | |
| But did not kill their first born | - Dayeinu! | דַּיֵּנוּ. |

אִלּוּ עָשָׂה בֵאלֹהֵיהֶם,

וְלֹא הָרַג אֶת בְּכוֹרֵיהֶם,

| If he killed their first born | | |
| But did not give us their possessions | - Dayeinu! | דַּיֵּנוּ. |

אִלּוּ הָרַג אֶת בְּכוֹרֵיהֶם

וְלֹא נָתַן לָנוּ אֶת מָמוֹנָם,

| If he gave us their possessions | | |
| But did not split the sea for us | - Dayeinu! | דַּיֵּנוּ. |

אִלּוּ נָתַן לָנוּ אֶת מָמוֹנָם

וְלֹא קָרַע לָנוּ אֶת הַיָּם,

| If he split the sea for us | | |
| But did not bring us through it on dry land | - Dayeinu! | דַּיֵּנוּ. |

אִלּוּ קָרַע לָנוּ אֶת הַיָּם

וְלֹא הֶעֱבִירָנוּ בְּתוֹכוֹ בֶּחָרָבָה,

| If he brought us through on dry land | | |
| But did not drown our enemies in it | - Dayeinu! | דַּיֵּנוּ. |

אִלּוּ הֶעֱבִירָנוּ בְּתוֹכוֹ בֶּחָרָבָה

וְלֹא שִׁקַּע צָרֵנוּ בְּתוֹכוֹ

| If he drowned our enemies in it | | |
| But did not provide for us 40 years in the desert | - Dayeinu! | דַּיֵּנוּ. |

אִלּוּ שִׁקַּע צָרֵנוּ בְּתוֹכוֹ

וְלֹא סִפֵּק צָרְכֵּנוּ בּמִדְבָּר אַרְבָּעִים שָׁנָה

| If he provided for us 40 years in the desert | | |
| But did not give us manna | - Dayeinu! | דַּיֵּנוּ. |

אִלּוּ סִפֵּק צָרְכֵּנוּ בּמִדְבָּר אַרְבָּעִים שָׁנָה

ולא הֶאֱכִילָנוּ אֶת הַמָּן

| If he gave us the manna | | |
| But did not give us the Shabbat | - Dayeinu! | דַּיֵּנוּ. |

אִלּוּ הֶאֱכִילָנוּ אֶת הַמָּן

וְלֹא נָתַן לָנוּ אֶת הַשַּׁבָּת,

| If he gave us the Shabbat | | |
| But did not bring us to Mt. Sinai | - Dayeinu! | דַּיֵּנוּ. |

אִלּוּ נָתַן לָנוּ אֶת הַשַּׁבָּת,

וְלֹא קֵרְבָנוּ לִפְנֵי הַר סִינַי,

| If he brought us to Mt. Sinai | | |
| But did not give us the Torah | - Dayeinu! | דַּיֵּנוּ. |

אִלּוּ קֵרְבָנוּ לִפְנֵי הַר סִינַי,

וְלֹא נָתַן לָנוּ אֶת הַתּוֹרָה.

| If he gave us the Torah | | |
| But did not bring us into the land of Israel | - Dayeinu! | דַּיֵּנוּ. |

אִלּוּ נָתַן לָנוּ אֶת הַתּוֹרָה

וְלֹא הִכְנִיסָנוּ לְאֶרֶץ יִשְׂרָאֵל,

| If he brought us into the land of Israel | | |
| But did not build for us the holy temple | - Dayeinu! | דַּיֵּנוּ. |

אִלּוּ הִכְנִיסָנוּ לְאֶרֶץ יִשְׂרָאֵל

וְלֹא בָנָה לָנוּ אֶת בֵּית הַבְּחִירָה

For how much goodness do we owe thanks to God?

He took us out of Egypt, Passed judgment against them, Acted against their Gods, Killed their first born, Gave us their possessions, Split the sea for us, Brought us through on dry land, Drowned our enemies in it, Provided for us for 40 years in the desert, Fed us the manna, Gave us the Shabbat, Brought us to Mt. Sinai, Gave us the Torah, Brought us into the land of Israel, Built us his holy temple to atone for all of our sins.

עַל אַחַת, כַּמָּה וְכַמָּה, טוֹבָה כְפוּלָה וּמְכֻפֶּלֶת לַמָּקוֹם עָלֵינוּ:

שֶׁהוֹצִיאָנוּ מִמִּצְרַיִם, וְעָשָׂה בָהֶם שְׁפָטִים, וְעָשָׂה בֵאלֹהֵיהֶם, וְהָרַג אֶת בְּכוֹרֵיהֶם, וְנָתַן לָנוּ אֶת מָמוֹנָם, וְקָרַע לָנוּ אֶת הַיָּם, וְהֶעֱבִירָנוּ בְּתוֹכוֹ בֶּחָרָבָה, וְשִׁקַּע צָרֵנוּ בְּתוֹכוֹ, וְסִפֵּק צָרְכֵּנוּ בְּמִדְבָּר אַרְבָּעִים שָׁנָה, וְהֶאֱכִילָנוּ אֶת הַמָּן, וְנָתַן לָנוּ אֶת הַשַּׁבָּת, וְקֵרְבָנוּ לִפְנֵי הַר סִינַי, וְנָתַן לָנוּ אֶת הַתּוֹרָה, וְהִכְנִיסָנוּ לְאֶרֶץ יִשְׂרָאֵל, וּבָנָה לָנוּ אֶת בֵּית הַבְּחִירָה לְכַפֵּר עַל כָּל עֲוֹנוֹתֵינוּ.

Rabban Gamliel said:

Whoever does not say these three things on Passover has not fulfilled his obligation:

The Passover Offering

Matza

The Bitter Herb

רַבָּן גַּמְלִיאֵל הָיָה אוֹמֵר:

כָּל שֶׁלֹּא אָמַר שְׁלֹשָׁה דְּבָרִים אֵלּוּ בְּפֶסַח, לֹא יָצָא יְדֵי חוֹבָתוֹ, וְאֵלּוּ הֵן:

פֶּסַח

מַצָּה

וּמָרוֹר

The Passover Offering

We do not lift the shank bone.

What was the reason for Passover offering that our ancestors ate in the time of the temple? It was because the Holy One, blessed be he, passed over the houses of our ancestors in Egypt. As it says: And you will say, this is a Passover offering to God, who passed over the houses of the children of Israel in Egypt as he struck the Egyptians and saved our homes, and the nation bowed to the ground (Exodus 12:26-27).

פֶּסַח שֶׁהָיוּ אֲבוֹתֵינוּ אוֹכְלִים בִּזְמַן שֶׁבֵּית הַמִּקְדָּשׁ הָיָה קַיָּם, עַל שׁוּם מָה? עַל שׁוּם שֶׁפֶּסַח הַקָּדוֹשׁ בָּרוּךְ הוּא עַל בָּתֵּי אֲבוֹתֵינוּ בְּמִצְרַיִם, שֶׁנֶּאֱמַר: וַאֲמַרְתֶּם זֶבַח פֶּסַח הוּא לַיי, אֲשֶׁר פָּסַח עַל בָּתֵּי בְּנֵי יִשְׂרָאֵל בְּמִצְרַיִם בְּנָגְפּוֹ אֶת מִצְרַיִם, וְאֶת בָּתֵּינוּ הִצִּיל? וַיִּקֹּד הָעָם וַיִּשְׁתַּחֲווּ.

Matzah

We raise the matzah from the seder plate.

What is the reason for the matzah that we eat? It is because the dough of our ancestors did not have time to rise before the king of kings, the Holy One, blessed be he, revealed himself to them and redeemed them. As it says: They baked the dough that they took out of Egypt into matzah, not chametz. Because they were sent out of Egypt and could not delay, and they had not prepared any supplies (Exodus 12:39).

מַצָּה זוֹ שֶׁאָנוּ אוֹכְלִים, עַל שׁוּם מַה? עַל שׁוּם שֶׁלֹּא הִסְפִּיק בְּצֵקָם שֶׁל אֲבוֹתֵינוּ לְהַחֲמִיץ עַד שֶׁנִּגְלָה עֲלֵיהֶם מֶלֶךְ מַלְכֵי הַמְּלָכִים, הַקָּדוֹשׁ בָּרוּךְ הוּא, וּגְאָלָם, שֶׁנֶּאֱמַר: וַיֹּאפוּ אֶת הַבָּצֵק אֲשֶׁר הוֹצִיאוּ מִמִּצְרַיִם עֻגֹת מַצּוֹת, כִּי לֹא חָמֵץ, כִּי גֹרְשׁוּ מִמִּצְרַיִם וְלֹא יָכְלוּ לְהִתְמַהְמֵהַּ, וְגַם צֵדָה לֹא עָשׂוּ לָהֶם.

The Bitter Herb

We raise the bitter herb from the seder plate.

What is the reason for the bitter herb that we eat? It is because the Egyptians made the lives of our ancestors in Egypt bitter, as it says: They embittered their lives with hard work, bricks and mortar, and all manner of work in the fields. All of their work was back breaking (Exodus 1:14)

מָרוֹר זֶה שֶׁאָנוּ אוֹכְלִים, עַל שׁוּם מַה? עַל שׁוּם שֶׁמֵּרְרוּ הַמִּצְרִים אֶת חַיֵּי אֲבוֹתֵינוּ בְּמִצְרַיִם, שֶׁנֶּאֱמַר: וַיְמָרְרוּ אֶת חַיֵּיהֶם בַּעֲבֹדָה קָשָׁה, בְּחֹמֶר וּבִלְבֵנִים וּבְכָל עֲבֹדָה בַּשָּׂדֶה אֵת כָּל עֲבֹדָתָם אֲשֶׁר עָבְדוּ בָהֶם בְּפָרֶךְ.

What Can We Do?

In every generation a person must view himself as though he personally went out from Egypt, as it says: You shall tell your son on that day, because of this God did for me, when I went out of Egypt (Exodus 12:8). The Holy One, blessed is he, did not just redeem our ancestors. Rather he redeemed us with them, as it says: He took us from there, to bring us, and to give us the land that he swore to our ancestors (Deuteronomy 6:23).

בְּכָל דוֹר וָדוֹר חַיָּב אָדָם לִרְאוֹת אֶת עַצְמוֹ כְּאִלּוּ הוּא יָצָא מִמִּצְרַים, שֶׁנֶּאֱמַר: וְהִגַּדְתָּ לְבִנְךָ בַּיּוֹם הַהוּא לֵאמר, בַּעֲבוּר זֶה עָשָׂה יי לִי בְּצֵאתִי מִמִּצְרָים. לֹא אֶת אֲבוֹתֵינוּ בִּלְבָד גָּאַל הַקָּדוֹשׁ בָּרוּךְ הוּא, אֶלָּא אַף אוֹתָנוּ גָּאַל עִמָּהֶם, שֶׁנֶּאֱמַר: וְאוֹתָנוּ הוֹצִיא מִשָּׁם, לְמַעַן הָבִיא אֹתָנוּ, לָתֶת לָנוּ אֶת הָאָרֶץ אֲשֶׁר נִשְׁבַּע לַאֲבֹתֵנוּ.

'Never doubt that a small group of thoughtful, committed citizens can change the world; indeed, it's the only thing that ever has.'

Margaret Mead, American anthropologist

We All Must Try

Rabbi Tarfon used to say: It is not your duty to complete the task, but neither are you at liberty to neglect it.

– Avot 2:16

What Can We Do?

Since human rights issues often depend on governments, it's difficult for individual citizens to make a difference. But as voters, consumers, and advocates, we can try to have an impact. What things can we do to further human rights?

Therefore it is our duty to thank and praise, pay tribute and glorify, exalt and honor, bless and acclaim the One who performed all these miracles for our fathers and for us. He took us out of slavery into freedom, out of grief into joy, out of mourning into a festival, out of darkness into a great light, out of slavery into redemption. We will recite a new song before Him! Halleluyah!

לְפִיכָךְ אֲנַחְנוּ חַיָּבִים לְהוֹדוֹת, לְהַלֵּל, לְשַׁבֵּחַ, לְפָאֵר, לְרוֹמֵם, לְהַדֵּר, לְבָרֵךְ, לְעַלֵּה וּלְקַלֵּס לְמִי שֶׁעָשָׂה לַאֲבוֹתֵינוּ וְלָנוּ אֶת כָּל הַנִּסִּים הָאֵלּוּ: הוֹצִיאָנוּ מֵעַבְדוּת לְחֵרוּת מִיָּגוֹן לְשִׂמְחָה, וּמֵאֵבֶל לְיוֹם טוֹב, וּמֵאֲפֵלָה לְאוֹר גָּדוֹל, וּמִשִּׁעְבּוּד לִגְאֻלָּה. וְנֹאמַר לְפָנָיו שִׁירָה חֲדָשָׁה: הַלְלוּיָהּ.

Praise the Lord! Praise, you servants of the Lord, praise the name of the Lord. Blessed be the name of the Lord from this time forth and forever. From the rising of the sun to its setting, the Lord's name is to be praised. High above all nations is the Lord; above the heavens is His glory. Who is like the Lord our God, who though enthroned on high, looks down upon heaven and earth? He raises the poor man out of the dust and lifts the needy one out of the trash heap, to seat them with nobles, with the nobles of His people. He turns the barren wife into a happy mother of children. Halleluyah! (Psalm 113)

הַלְלוּיָהּ הַלְלוּ עַבְדֵי יְהוָה הַלְלוּ אֶת שֵׁם יְהוָה. יְהִי שֵׁם יְהוָה מְבֹרָךְ מֵעַתָּה וְעַד עוֹלָם. מִמִּזְרַח שֶׁמֶשׁ עַד מְבוֹאוֹ מְהֻלָּל שֵׁם יְהוָה. רָם עַל כָּל גּוֹיִם יְהוָה עַל הַשָּׁמַיִם כְּבוֹדוֹ. מִי כַּיהוָה אֱלֹהֵינוּ הַמַּגְבִּיהִי לָשָׁבֶת. הַמַּשְׁפִּילִי לִרְאוֹת בַּשָּׁמַיִם וּבָאָרֶץ. מְקִימִי מֵעָפָר דָּל מֵאַשְׁפֹּת יָרִים אֶבְיוֹן. לְהוֹשִׁיבִי עִם נְדִיבִים עִם נְדִיבֵי עַמּוֹ. מוֹשִׁיבִי עֲקֶרֶת הַבַּיִת אֵם הַבָּנִים שְׂמֵחָה הַלְלוּיָהּ.

When Israel went out of Egypt, Jacob's household from a people of strange speech, Judah became God's sanctuary, Israel His kingdom. The sea saw it and fled; the Jordan turned backward. The mountains skipped like rams, and the hills like lambs. Why is it, sea, that you flee? Why, O Jordan, do you turn backward? You mountains, why do you skip like rams? You hills, why do you leap like lambs? O earth, tremble at the Lord's presence, at the presence of the God of Jacob, who turns the rock into a pond of water, the flint into a flowing fountain. (Psalm 114)

בְּצֵאת יִשְׂרָאֵל מִמִּצְרַיִם בֵּית יַעֲקֹב מֵעַם לֹעֵז. הָיְתָה יְהוּדָה לְקָדְשׁוֹ יִשְׂרָאֵל מַמְשְׁלוֹתָיו. הַיָּם רָאָה וַיָּנֹס הַיַּרְדֵּן יִסֹּב לְאָחוֹר. הֶהָרִים רָקְדוּ כְאֵילִים גְּבָעוֹת כִּבְנֵי צֹאן. מַה לְּךָ הַיָּם כִּי תָנוּס הַיַּרְדֵּן תִּסֹּב לְאָחוֹר. הֶהָרִים תִּרְקְדוּ כְאֵילִים גְּבָעוֹת כִּבְנֵי צֹאן. מִלִּפְנֵי אָדוֹן חוּלִי אָרֶץ מִלִּפְנֵי אֱלוֹהַּ יַעֲקֹב. הַהֹפְכִי הַצּוּר אֲגַם מָיִם חַלָּמִישׁ לְמַעְיְנוֹ מָיִם.

The Second Cup

Over the second cup of wine, we recite:

Blessed art Thou, Lord our God, King of the universe, who has redeemed us and our fathers from Egypt and enabled us to reach this night that we may eat matzah and marror. So Lord our God and God of our fathers, enable us to reach future holidays and festivals in peace, rejoicing in the rebuilding of Zion thy city, and joyful at thy service. There we shall eat of the offerings and Passover sacrifices [On Saturday night read: of the Passover sacrifices and offerings] which will be placed upon thy altar. We shall sing a new hymn of praise to You for our redemption and for our liberation. Blessed art Thou, O Lord, who has redeemed Israel.

Blessed art Thou, Lord our God, King of the universe, who createst the fruit of the vine.

בָּרוּךְ אַתָּה יְיָ אֱלֹהֵינוּ מֶלֶךְ הָעוֹלָם, אֲשֶׁר גְּאָלָנוּ וְגָאַל אֶת אֲבוֹתֵינוּ מִמִּצְרַיִם, וְהִגִּיעָנוּ לַלַּיְלָה הַזֶּה לֶאֱכָל בּוֹ מַצָּה וּמָרוֹר. כֵּן יְיָ אֱלֹהֵינוּ וֵאלֹהֵי אֲבוֹתֵינוּ יַגִּיעֵנוּ לְמוֹעֲדִים וְלִרְגָלִים אֲחֵרִים הַבָּאִים לִקְרָאתֵנוּ לְשָׁלוֹם, שְׂמֵחִים בְּבִנְיַן עִירֶךָ וְשָׂשִׂים בַּעֲבוֹדָתֶךָ. וְנֹאכַל שָׁם מִן הַזְּבָחִים וּמִן הַפְּסָחִים [במוצאי שבת: מִן הַפְּסָחִים וּמִן הַזְּבָחִים] אֲשֶׁר יַגִּיעַ דָּמָם עַל קִיר מִזְבַּחֲךָ לְרָצוֹן, וְנוֹדֶה לְךָ שִׁיר חָדָשׁ עַל גְּאֻלָּתֵנוּ וְעַל פְּדוּת נַפְשֵׁנוּ. בָּרוּךְ אַתָּה יְיָ גָּאַל יִשְׂרָאֵל.

בָּרוּךְ אַתָּה יְיָ אֱלֹהֵינוּ מֶלֶךְ הָעוֹלָם בּוֹרֵא פְּרִי הַגָּפֶן.

We drink the second cup of wine while reclining.

Rachtza

רָחְצָה

Washing hands for the meal

After washing we recite the blessing:

Blessed art Thou, Lord our God, King of the universe, who hast sanctified us with thy commandments, and commanded us concerning the washing of the hands.

בָּרוּךְ אַתָּה יְיָ אֱלֹהֵינוּ מֶלֶךְ הָעוֹלָם, אֲשֶׁר קִדְּשָׁנוּ בְּמִצְוֹתָיו וְצִוָּנוּ עַל נְטִילַת יָדַיִם.

Motze Matzah

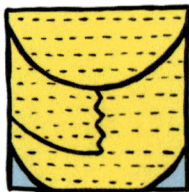

מוֹצִיא מַצָּה

Eating the Matzah

Holding all three Matzah we recite:

Blessed art Thou, Lord our God, King of the universe, who bringest forth bread from the earth.

בָּרוּךְ אַתָּה יְיָ, אֱלֹהֵינוּ מֶלֶךְ הָעוֹלָם, הַמּוֹצִיא לֶחֶם מִן הָאָרֶץ:

Holding the top two Matzah we recite:

Blessed art Thou, Lord our God, King of the universe, who hast sanctified us with thy commandments, and commanded us concerning the eating of matzah.

בָּרוּךְ אַתָּה יְיָ, אֱלֹהֵינוּ מֶלֶךְ הָעוֹלָם, אֲשֶׁר קִדְּשָׁנוּ בְּמִצְוֹתָיו וְצִוָּנוּ עַל אֲכִילַת מַצָּה:

We eat our portion of Matzah

Maror

מָרוֹר

The Bitter Herb

We dip a portion of the bitter herb in charoset and say:

Blessed art Thou, Lord our God, King of the universe, who hast sanctified us with thy commandments, and commanded us concerning the eating of the bitter herbs.

בָּרוּךְ אַתָּה יְיָ אֱלֹהֵינוּ מֶלֶךְ הָעוֹלָם, אֲשֶׁר קִדְּשָׁנוּ בְּמִצְוֹתָיו וְצִוָּנוּ עַל אֲכִילַת מָרוֹר.

Korech

כּוֹרֵךְ

The Hillel Sandwich

We combine matzah, bitter herb, and charoset and say:

To remind us of the Temple we do as Hillel did in Temple times; he combined matzo and marror in a sandwich and ate them together, to fulfill what is written in the Torah: "They shall eat it with unleavened bread and bitter herbs."

זֵכֶר לְמִקְדָּשׁ כְּהִלֵּל: כֵּן עָשָׂה

הִלֵּל בִּזְמַן שֶׁבֵּית הַמִּקְדָּשׁ הָיָה

קַיָם. הָיָה כּוֹרֵךְ פֶּסַח מַצָּה וּמָרוֹר

וְאוֹכֵל בְּיַחַד. לְקַיֵּם מַה שֶׁנֶּאֱמַר:

עַל־מַצוֹת וּמְרוֹרִים יֹאכְלֻהוּ:

Shulchan Orech

שֻׁלְחָן עוֹרֵךְ

The Festive Meal

The holiday meal is served

Tzafun

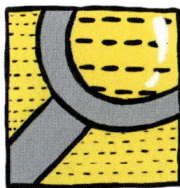

צָפוּן

The Afikoman

The afikoman is eaten at the conclusion of the meal.
Often it is lost and found by the children, who are given a prize for finding it.

Barech

בָּרֵךְ

We pour the third cup of wine and recite Grace after the meal

שִׁיר הַמַּעֲלוֹת בְּשׁוּב יְיָ אֶת שִׁיבַת צִיּוֹן הָיִינוּ כְּחֹלְמִים. אָז יִמָּלֵא שְׂחוֹק פִּינוּ וּלְשׁוֹנֵנוּ רִנָּה אָז יֹאמְרוּ בַגּוֹיִם הִגְדִּיל יְיָ לַעֲשׂוֹת עִם אֵלֶּה. הִגְדִּיל יְיָ לַעֲשׂוֹת עִמָּנוּ הָיִינוּ שְׂמֵחִים. שׁוּבָה יְיָ אֶת שְׁבִיתֵנוּ כַּאֲפִיקִים בַּנֶּגֶב. הַזֹּרְעִים בְּדִמְעָה בְּרִנָּה יִקְצֹרוּ. הָלוֹךְ יֵלֵךְ וּבָכֹה נֹשֵׂא מֶשֶׁךְ הַזָּרַע בֹּא יָבוֹא בְרִנָּה נֹשֵׂא אֲלֻמֹּתָיו.

הַמְזַמֵּן: רַבּוֹתַי, נְבָרֵךְ!
הַמְסֻבִּין: יְהִי שֵׁם יְיָ מְבֹרָךְ מֵעַתָּה וְעַד עוֹלָם.
הַמְזַמֵּן: בִּרְשׁוּת מָרָנָן וְרַבָּנָן וְרַבּוֹתַי,
נְבָרֵךְ (אֱלֹהֵינוּ) שֶׁאָכַלְנוּ מִשֶּׁלוֹ.
הַמְסֻבִּין: בָּרוּךְ (אֱלֹהֵינוּ) שֶׁאָכַלְנוּ
מִשֶּׁלוֹ וּבְטוּבוֹ חָיִינוּ.
הַמְזַמֵּן: בָּרוּךְ (אֱלֹהֵינוּ) שֶׁאָכַלְנוּ מִשֶּׁלוֹ
וּבְטוּבוֹ חָיִינוּ.
בָּרוּךְ הוּא וּבָרוּךְ שְׁמוֹ:

בָּרוּךְ אַתָּה יְיָ אֱלֹהֵינוּ מֶלֶךְ הָעוֹלָם, הַזָּן אֶת הָעוֹלָם כֻּלּוֹ בְּטוּבוֹ בְּחֵן בְּחֶסֶד וּבְרַחֲמִים, הוּא נֹתֵן לֶחֶם לְכָל-בָּשָׂר כִּי לְעוֹלָם חַסְדּוֹ, וּבְטוּבוֹ הַגָּדוֹל תָּמִיד לֹא חָסַר לָנוּ וְאַל יֶחְסַר לָנוּ מָזוֹן לְעוֹלָם וָעֶד, בַּעֲבוּר שְׁמוֹ הַגָּדוֹל, כִּי הוּא אֵל זָן וּמְפַרְנֵס לַכֹּל, וּמֵטִיב לַכֹּל וּמֵכִין מָזוֹן לְכָל בְּרִיּוֹתָיו אֲשֶׁר בָּרָא. בָּרוּךְ אַתָּה יְיָ הַזָּן אֶת הַכֹּל.

נוֹדֶה לְךָ יְיָ אֱלֹהֵינוּ עַל שֶׁהִנְחַלְתָּ לַאֲבוֹתֵינוּ אֶרֶץ חֶמְדָּה טוֹבָה וּרְחָבָה, וְעַל שֶׁהוֹצֵאתָנוּ יְיָ אֱלֹהֵינוּ מֵאֶרֶץ מִצְרַיִם וּפְדִיתָנוּ מִבֵּית עֲבָדִים, וְעַל בְּרִיתְךָ שֶׁחָתַמְתָּ בִּבְשָׂרֵנוּ וְעַל תּוֹרָתְךָ שֶׁלִּמַּדְתָּנוּ וְעַל חֻקֶּיךָ שֶׁהוֹדַעְתָּנוּ, וְעַל חַיִּים חֵן וָחֶסֶד שֶׁחוֹנַנְתָּנוּ, וְעַל אֲכִילַת מָזוֹן שָׁאַתָּה זָן וּמְפַרְנֵס אוֹתָנוּ תָּמִיד, בְּכָל יוֹם וּבְכָל עֵת וּבְכָל שָׁעָה.

וְעַל הַכֹּל יְיָ אֱלֹהֵינוּ אֲנַחְנוּ מוֹדִים לָךְ וּמְבָרְכִים אוֹתָךְ, יִתְבָּרַךְ שִׁמְךָ בְּפִי כָּל חַי תָּמִיד לְעוֹלָם וָעֶד, כַּכָּתוּב: "וְאָכַלְתָּ וְשָׂבָעְתָּ, וּבֵרַכְתָּ אֶת יְיָ אֱלֹהֶיךָ עַל הָאָרֶץ הַטּוֹבָה אֲשֶׁר נָתַן לָךְ". בָּרוּךְ אַתָּה יְיָ, עַל הָאָרֶץ וְעַל הַמָּזוֹן.

רַחֶם נָא יְיָ אֱלֹהֵינוּ עַל יִשְׂרָאֵל עַמֶּךָ, וְעַל יְרוּשָׁלַיִם עִירֶךָ, וְעַל צִיּוֹן מִשְׁכַּן כְּבוֹדֶךָ, וְעַל מַלְכוּת בֵּית דָּוִד מְשִׁיחֶךָ, וְעַל הַבַּיִת הַגָּדוֹל וְהַקָּדוֹשׁ שֶׁנִּקְרָא שִׁמְךָ עָלָיו. אֱלֹהֵינוּ, אָבִינוּ, רְעֵנוּ, זוּנֵנוּ, פַּרְנְסֵנוּ וְכַלְכְּלֵנוּ וְהַרְוִיחֵנוּ, וְהַרְוַח לָנוּ יְיָ אֱלֹהֵינוּ מְהֵרָה מִכָּל צָרוֹתֵינוּ. וְנָא אַל תַּצְרִיכֵנוּ יְיָ אֱלֹהֵינוּ, לֹא לִידֵי מַתְּנַת בָּשָׂר וָדָם וְלֹא לִידֵי הַלְוָאָתָם, כִּי אִם לְיָדְךָ הַמְּלֵאָה הַפְּתוּחָה הַקְּדוֹשָׁה וְהָרְחָבָה, שֶׁלֹּא נֵבוֹשׁ וְלֹא נִכָּלֵם לְעוֹלָם וָעֶד.

רְצֵה וְהַחֲלִיצֵנוּ יְיָ אֱלֹהֵינוּ בְּמִצְוֹתֶיךָ וּבְמִצְוַת יוֹם הַשְּׁבִיעִי הַשַּׁבָּת הַגָּדוֹל וְהַקָּדוֹשׁ הַזֶּה. כִּי יוֹם זֶה גָּדוֹל וְקָדוֹשׁ הוּא לְפָנֶיךָ לִשְׁבָּת בּוֹ וְלָנוּחַ בּוֹ בְּאַהֲבָה כְּמִצְוַת רְצוֹנֶךָ. וּבִרְצוֹנְךָ הָנִיחַ לָנוּ יְיָ אֱלֹהֵינוּ שֶׁלֹּא תְהֵא צָרָה וְיָגוֹן וַאֲנָחָה בְּיוֹם מְנוּחָתֵנוּ. וְהַרְאֵנוּ יְיָ אֱלֹהֵינוּ בְּנֶחָמַת צִיּוֹן עִירֶךָ וּבְבִנְיַן יְרוּשָׁלַיִם עִיר קָדְשֶׁךָ כִּי אַתָּה הוּא בַּעַל הַיְשׁוּעוֹת וּבַעַל הַנֶּחָמוֹת.

אֱלֹהֵינוּ וֵאלֹהֵי אֲבוֹתֵינוּ, יַעֲלֶה וְיָבוֹא וְיַגִּיעַ, וְיֵרָאֶה וְיֵרָצֶה וְיִשָּׁמַע, וְיִפָּקֵד וְיִזָּכֵר זִכְרוֹנֵנוּ וּפִקְדוֹנֵנוּ וְזִכְרוֹן אֲבוֹתֵינוּ, וְזִכְרוֹן מָשִׁיחַ בֶּן דָּוִד עַבְדֶּךָ, וְזִכְרוֹן יְרוּשָׁלַיִם עִיר קָדְשֶׁךָ, וְזִכְרוֹן כָּל עַמְּךָ בֵּית יִשְׂרָאֵל לְפָנֶיךָ לִפְלֵטָה, לְטוֹבָה, לְחֵן וּלְחֶסֶד וּלְרַחֲמִים, לְחַיִּים וּלְשָׁלוֹם, בְּיוֹם חַג הַמַּצּוֹת הַזֶּה. זָכְרֵנוּ יְיָ אֱלֹהֵינוּ בּוֹ לְטוֹבָה, וּפָקְדֵנוּ בוֹ לִבְרָכָה, וְהוֹשִׁיעֵנוּ בוֹ לְחַיִּים וּבִדְבַר יְשׁוּעָה וְרַחֲמִים חוּס וְחָנֵּנוּ, וְרַחֵם עָלֵינוּ וְהוֹשִׁיעֵנוּ, כִּי אֵלֶיךָ עֵינֵינוּ, כִּי אֵל מֶלֶךְ חַנּוּן וְרַחוּם אָתָּה.

וּבְנֵה יְרוּשָׁלַיִם עִיר הַקֹּדֶשׁ בִּמְהֵרָה בְיָמֵינוּ. בָּרוּךְ אַתָּה יְיָ, בּוֹנֶה בְרַחֲמָיו יְרוּשָׁלָיִם. אָמֵן.

בָּרוּךְ אַתָּה יְיָ, אֱלֹהֵינוּ מֶלֶךְ הָעוֹלָם, הָאֵל אָבִינוּ, מַלְכֵּנוּ, אַדִּירֵנוּ, בּוֹרְאֵנוּ, גּוֹאֲלֵנוּ, יוֹצְרֵנוּ, קְדוֹשֵׁנוּ קְדוֹשׁ יַעֲקֹב, רוֹעֵנוּ רוֹעֵה יִשְׂרָאֵל, הַמֶּלֶךְ הַטּוֹב וְהַמֵּיטִיב לַכֹּל, שֶׁבְּכָל יוֹם וָיוֹם הוּא הֵיטִיב, הוּא מֵיטִיב, הוּא יֵיטִיב לָנוּ. הוּא גְמָלָנוּ הוּא גוֹמְלֵנוּ הוּא יִגְמְלֵנוּ לָעַד, לְחֵן וּלְחֶסֶד וּלְרַחֲמִים וּלְרֶוַח הַצָּלָה וְהַצְלָחָה, בְּרָכָה וִישׁוּעָה, נֶחָמָה פַּרְנָסָה וְכַלְכָּלָה, וְרַחֲמִים וְחַיִּים וְשָׁלוֹם וְכָל טוֹב; וּמִכָּל טוֹב לְעוֹלָם אַל יְחַסְּרֵנוּ.

הָרַחֲמָן הוּא יִמְלוֹךְ עָלֵינוּ לְעוֹלָם וָעֶד. הָרַחֲמָן הוּא יִתְבָּרַךְ בַּשָּׁמַיִם וּבָאָרֶץ. הָרַחֲמָן הוּא יִשְׁתַּבַּח לְדוֹר דּוֹרִים, וְיִתְפָּאַר בָּנוּ לָעַד וּלְנֵצַח נְצָחִים, וְיִתְהַדַּר בָּנוּ לָעַד וּלְעוֹלְמֵי עוֹלָמִים. הָרַחֲמָן הוּא יְפַרְנְסֵנוּ בְּכָבוֹד. הָרַחֲמָן הוּא יִשְׁבּוֹר עֻלֵּנוּ מֵעַל צַוָּארֵנוּ, וְהוּא יוֹלִיכֵנוּ קוֹמְמִיּוּת לְאַרְצֵנוּ. הָרַחֲמָן הוּא יִשְׁלַח לָנוּ בְּרָכָה מְרֻבָּה בַּבַּיִת הַזֶּה, וְעַל שֻׁלְחָן זֶה שֶׁאָכַלְנוּ עָלָיו. הָרַחֲמָן הוּא יִשְׁלַח לָנוּ אֶת אֵלִיָּהוּ הַנָּבִיא זָכוּר לַטּוֹב, וִיבַשֶּׂר לָנוּ בְּשׂוֹרוֹת טוֹבוֹת יְשׁוּעוֹת וְנֶחָמוֹת.

הָרַחֲמָן, הוּא יְבָרֵךְ אֶת (אָבִי מוֹרִי) בַּעַל הַבַּיִת הַזֶּה, וְאֶת (אִמִּי מוֹרָתִי) בַּעֲלַת הַבַּיִת הַזֶּה, הָרַחֲמָן, הוּא יְבָרֵךְ אוֹתִי (וְאִשְׁתִּי וְזַרְעִי וְאֶת כָּל אֲשֶׁר לִי).

הָרַחֲמָן, הוּא יְבָרֵךְ אֶת בַּעַל הַבַּיִת הַזֶּה, וְאֶת אִשְׁתּוֹ בַּעֲלַת הַבַּיִת הַזֶּה. אוֹתָם וְאֶת בֵּיתָם וְאֶת זַרְעָם וְאֶת כָּל אֲשֶׁר לָהֶם אוֹתָנוּ וְאֶת כָּל אֲשֶׁר לָנוּ, כְּמוֹ שֶׁנִּתְבָּרְכוּ אֲבוֹתֵינוּ, אַבְרָהָם יִצְחָק וְיַעֲקֹב: בַּכֹּל, מִכֹּל, כֹּל. כֵּן יְבָרֵךְ אוֹתָנוּ וְכֻלָּנוּ יַחַד. בִּבְרָכָה שְׁלֵמָה, וְנֹאמַר אָמֵן:

בַּמָּרוֹם יְלַמְּדוּ עֲלֵיהֶם וְעָלֵינוּ זְכוּת שֶׁתְּהֵא לְמִשְׁמֶרֶת שָׁלוֹם. וְנִשָּׂא בְרָכָה מֵאֵת יְיָ, וּצְדָקָה מֵאֱלֹהֵי יִשְׁעֵנוּ, וְנִמְצָא חֵן וְשֵׂכֶל טוֹב בְּעֵינֵי אֱלֹהִים וְאָדָם.

הָרַחֲמָן הוּא יַנְחִילֵנוּ יוֹם שֶׁכֻּלּוֹ שַׁבָּת וּמְנוּחָה לְחַיֵּי הָעוֹלָמִים.

הָרַחֲמָן הוּא יַנְחִילֵנוּ יוֹם שֶׁכֻּלּוֹ טוֹב. הָרַחֲמָן הוּא יְזַכֵּנוּ לִימוֹת הַמָּשִׁיחַ וּלְחַיֵּי הָעוֹלָם הַבָּא.

מִגְדּוֹל יְשׁוּעוֹת מַלְכּוֹ, וְעֹשֶׂה חֶסֶד לִמְשִׁיחוֹ, לְדָוִד וּלְזַרְעוֹ עַד עוֹלָם. עֹשֶׂה שָׁלוֹם בִּמְרוֹמָיו, הוּא יַעֲשֶׂה שָׁלוֹם עָלֵינוּ וְעַל כָּל יִשְׂרָאֵל. וְאִמְרוּ: אָמֵן.

יְראוּ אֶת יְיָ קְדֹשָׁיו, כִּי אֵין מַחְסוֹר לִירֵאָיו. כְּפִירִים רָשׁוּ וְרָעֵבוּ, וְדֹרְשֵׁי יְיָ לֹא יַחְסְרוּ כָל טוֹב. הוֹדוּ לַייָ כִּי טוֹב, כִּי לְעוֹלָם חַסְדּוֹ. פּוֹתֵחַ אֶת יָדֶךָ, וּמַשְׂבִּיעַ לְכָל חַי רָצוֹן. בָּרוּךְ הַגֶּבֶר אֲשֶׁר יִבְטַח בַּייָ, וְהָיָה יְיָ מִבְטַחוֹ. נַעַר הָיִיתִי גַם זָקַנְתִּי, וְלֹא רָאִיתִי צַדִּיק נֶעֱזָב, וְזַרְעוֹ מְבַקֶּשׁ לָחֶם. יְיָ עֹז לְעַמּוֹ יִתֵּן, יְיָ יְבָרֵךְ אֶת עַמּוֹ בַשָּׁלוֹם.

The Third Cup

Over the third cup of wine, we recite:

Blessed art Thou, Lord our God, King of the universe, who createst the fruit of the vine.

בָּרוּךְ אַתָּה יְיָ אֱלֹהֵינוּ מֶלֶךְ הָעוֹלָם בּוֹרֵא פְּרִי הַגָּפֶן.

We drink the third cup of wine while reclining.

Reprisals and International Justice

A cup of wine is poured in honor of the Prophet Elijah.
The door is opened and we say:

Pour out your wrath upon the nations that have not known you, and upon the kingdoms that do not call your name. For they have devoured Jacob and laid waste to his habitations. **Pour your fury upon them, let your blazing anger overtake them. Pursue them with hatred and may they be destroyed** from under God's heavens (Psalms 79:6-7)

שְׁפֹךְ חֲמָתְךָ אֶל הַגּוֹיִם אֲשֶׁר לֹא יְדָעוּךָ

וְעַל מַמְלָכוֹת אֲשֶׁר בְּשִׁמְךָ לֹא קָרָאוּ.

כִּי אָכַל אֶת יַעֲקֹב וְאֶת נָוֵהוּ הֵשַׁמּוּ.

שְׁפָךְ עֲלֵיהֶם זַעְמֶךָ וַחֲרוֹן אַפְּךָ יַשִּׂיגֵם.

תִּרְדֹּף בְּאַף וְתַשְׁמִידֵם מִתַּחַת שְׁמֵי יְיָ.

The International Criminal Court

In 1998 many nations collaborated to create the International Criminal Court (ICC) to punish individuals who commit war crimes, genocide, and crimes against humanity. The goal was to deter political and military leaders from committing these crimes due to fear that they themselves can now be put on trial and punished.

The preamble to the statute creating the ICC explains its purpose as follows:

Mindful that during this century millions of children, women and men have been victims of unimaginable atrocities that deeply shock the conscience of humanity.

Recognizing that such grave crimes threaten the peace, security and well-being of the world.

Affirming that the most serious crimes of concern to the international community as a whole must not go unpunished...

Determined to put an end to impunity for the perpetrators of these crimes and thus to contribute to the prevention of such crimes

The Guilty Must Be Punished

If someone is known to have committed a murder but there is not enough evidence to convict them in court. . . the king is allowed to put that person to death in order to make a better world. . .to instill fear and break the wicked.

– Maimonides Laws of Kings 3:10

Can there be International Justice?

Until creation of the ICC, threat of reprisal was the only way for one country to prevent another from violating international law. But the ICC has limited jurisdiction and limited means of enforcing its judgments. Many political and military leaders have been able to keep themselves beyond its reach even when indicted for committing grave violations of human rights.

Can we create a respected, impartial, and affective system of international justice that will deter war crimes and crimes against humanity? Or will the threat of reprisals always remain the best way for countries to protect their interests?

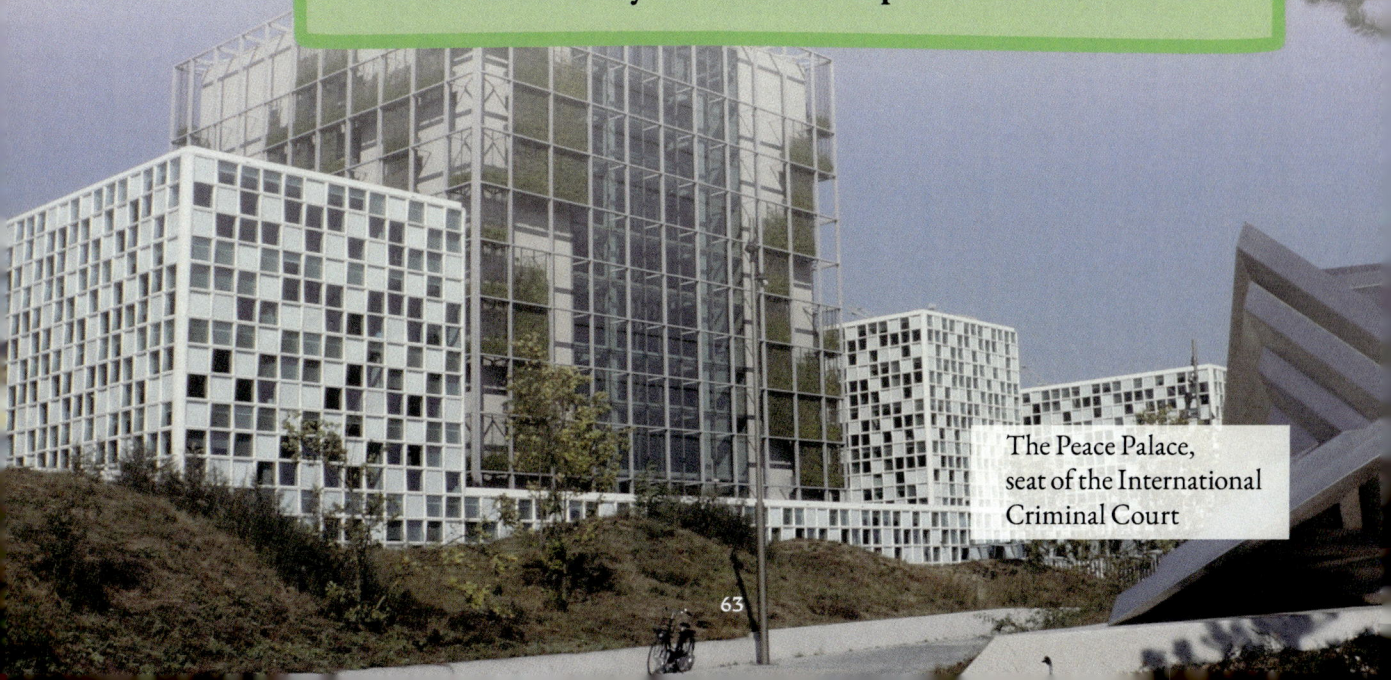

The Peace Palace, seat of the International Criminal Court

Hallel

We pour the fourth cup of wine and recite the Halel:

Nor for our sake, O Lord, not for our sake, but for thy name's sake give glory, because of thy kindness and thy truth. Why should the nations say: "Where is their God?" Our God is in the heavens; He does whatever He pleases! Their idols are silver and gold, the work of human hands. They have a mouth, but they cannot speak; they have eyes, but they cannot see; they have ears, but they cannot hear; they have a nose, but they cannot smell; they have hands, but they cannot feel; they have feet, but they cannot walk; nor can they utter a sound with their throat. Those who make them shall become like them, whoever trusts in them. O Israel, trust in the Lord! He is their help and shield. You who revere the Lord, trust in the Lord! He is their help and shield.

(Psalm 115:1-11)

The Lord who has remembered us will bless;

He will bless the house of Israel; He will bless the house of Aaron; He will bless those who revere the Lord, the small with the great. May the Lord increase you, you and your children. You are blessed by the Lord, who made the heaven and earth. The heaven is the Lord's heaven, but He has given the earth to mankind. The dead cannot praise the Lord, nor can any who go down into silence. We will bless the Lord from this time forth and forever. Halleluyah!

(Psalm 115:12-18)

I love that the Lord hears my supplications. Because He has inclined His ear to me, I will call upon Him as long as I live. The cords of death encircled me; the pains of the grave have overtaken me; I found trouble and sorrow. Then I called upon the name of the Lord:

לֹא לָנוּ יְיָ לֹא לָנוּ, כִּי לְשִׁמְךָ תֵּן כָּבוֹד, עַל חַסְדְּךָ, עַל אֲמִתֶּךָ. לָמָּה יֹאמְרוּ הַגּוֹיִם אַיֵּה נָא אֱלֹהֵיהֶם, וֵאלֹהֵינוּ בַשָּׁמַיִם, כֹּל אֲשֶׁר חָפֵץ עָשָׂה. עֲצַבֵּיהֶם כֶּסֶף וְזָהָב מַעֲשֵׂה יְדֵי אָדָם. פֶּה לָהֶם וְלֹא יְדַבֵּרוּ, עֵינַיִם לָהֶם וְלֹא יִרְאוּ. אָזְנַיִם לָהֶם וְלֹא יִשְׁמָעוּ, אַף לָהֶם וְלֹא יְרִיחוּן. יְדֵיהֶם וְלֹא יְמִישׁוּן, רַגְלֵיהֶם וְלֹא יְהַלֵּכוּ, לֹא יֶהְגּוּ בִּגְרוֹנָם. כְּמוֹהֶם יִהְיוּ עֹשֵׂיהֶם, כֹּל אֲשֶׁר בֹּטֵחַ בָּהֶם. יִשְׂרָאֵל בְּטַח בַּיְיָ, עֶזְרָם וּמָגִנָּם הוּא. בֵּית אַהֲרֹן בִּטְחוּ בַיְיָ, עֶזְרָם וּמָגִנָּם הוּא. יִרְאֵי יְיָ בִּטְחוּ בַיְיָ, עֶזְרָם וּמָגִנָּם הוּא.

יְיָ זְכָרָנוּ יְבָרֵךְ, יְבָרֵךְ אֶת בֵּית יִשְׂרָאֵל, יְבָרֵךְ אֶת בֵּית אַהֲרֹן. יְבָרֵךְ יִרְאֵי יְיָ, הַקְּטַנִּים עִם הַגְּדֹלִים. יֹסֵף יְיָ עֲלֵיכֶם, עֲלֵיכֶם וְעַל בְּנֵיכֶם. בְּרוּכִים אַתֶּם לַיְיָ, עֹשֵׂה שָׁמַיִם וָאָרֶץ. הַשָּׁמַיִם שָׁמַיִם לַיְיָ וְהָאָרֶץ נָתַן לִבְנֵי אָדָם. לֹא הַמֵּתִים יְהַלְלוּ יָהּ וְלֹא כָּל יֹרְדֵי דוּמָה. וַאֲנַחְנוּ נְבָרֵךְ יָהּ מֵעַתָּה וְעַד עוֹלָם. הַלְלוּיָהּ:

אָהַבְתִּי כִּי יִשְׁמַע יְיָ אֶת קוֹלִי, תַּחֲנוּנָי. כִּי הִטָּה אָזְנוֹ לִי וּבְיָמַי אֶקְרָא. אֲפָפוּנִי חֶבְלֵי מָוֶת וּמְצָרֵי שְׁאוֹל מְצָאוּנִי, צָרָה וְיָגוֹן אֶמְצָא. וּבְשֵׁם יְיָ אֶקְרָא, אָנָּא יְיָ מַלְּטָה

64

"O Lord, save my life!" Gracious is the Lord, and righteous and our God is merciful. The Lord protects the simple; I was brought low and He saved me. Return to thy rest, O my soul, for the Lord has been kind to you. Thou hast delivered my soul from death, my eyes from tears and my feet from stumbling. I shall walk before the Lord in the lands of the living. I kept faith even when I cry out: "I am greatly afflicted.' I said in haste: "All men are deceitful." (Psalm 116:1-11)

How can I repay the Lord for all His kind acts toward me? I will raise the cup of salvations, and call upon the name of the Lord. My vows to the Lord I will pay in the presence of all His people. Precious in the sight of the Lord is the death of His pious followers. Please, O Lord, I am truly thy servant; I am thy servant, the son of thy handmaid; Thou has loosened my bonds. To Thee I sacrifice a thanksgiving offering, and call upon the name of the Lord. My vows to the Lord I will pay in the presence of all His people, in the courts of the Lord's house, in the midst of Jerusalem. Halleluyah! (Psalm 116:12-19)

Give thanks to the Lord, all you nations; praise Him, all you peoples! For His kindness overwhelms us, and the truth of the Lord is forever, Halleluyah! (Psalm 117)

Give thanks to the Lord, for He is good;
His kindness endures forever.

Let Israel say:
His kindness endures forever.

Let the house of Aaron say:
His kindness endures forever.

Let those who revere the Lord say:
His kindness endures forever. (Psalm 118:1-4)

נַפְשִׁי. חַנּוּן יְיָ וְצַדִּיק, וֵאלֹהֵינוּ מְרַחֵם. שֹׁמֵר פְּתָאִים יְיָ, דַּלּוֹתִי וְלִי יְהוֹשִׁיעַ. שׁוּבִי נַפְשִׁי לִמְנוּחָיְכִי, כִּי יְיָ גָּמַל עָלָיְכִי. כִּי חִלַּצְתָּ נַפְשִׁי מִמָּוֶת, אֶת עֵינִי מִן דִּמְעָה, אֶת רַגְלִי מִדֶּחִי. אֶתְהַלֵּךְ לִפְנֵי יְיָ בְּאַרְצוֹת הַחַיִּים. הֶאֱמַנְתִּי כִּי אֲדַבֵּר, אֲנִי עָנִיתִי מְאֹד. אֲנִי אָמַרְתִּי בְחָפְזִי, כָּל הָאָדָם כֹּזֵב.

מָה אָשִׁיב לַיְיָ כָּל תַּגְמוּלוֹהִי עָלָי. כּוֹס יְשׁוּעוֹת אֶשָּׂא וּבְשֵׁם יְיָ אֶקְרָא. נְדָרַי לַיְיָ אֲשַׁלֵּם נֶגְדָה נָּא לְכָל עַמּוֹ. יָקָר בְּעֵינֵי יְיָ הַמָּוְתָה לַחֲסִידָיו. אָנָּא יְיָ כִּי אֲנִי עַבְדֶּךָ, אֲנִי עַבְדְּךָ בֶּן אֲמָתֶךָ, פִּתַּחְתָּ לְמוֹסֵרָי. לְךָ אֶזְבַּח זֶבַח תּוֹדָה וּבְשֵׁם יְיָ אֶקְרָא. נְדָרַי לַיְיָ אֲשַׁלֵּם נֶגְדָה נָּא לְכָל עַמּוֹ. בְּחַצְרוֹת בֵּית יְיָ, בְּתוֹכֵכִי יְרוּשָׁלָיִם, הַלְלוּיָהּ:

הַלְלוּ אֶת יְיָ כָּל גּוֹיִם, שַׁבְּחוּהוּ כָּל הָאֻמִּים. כִּי גָבַר עָלֵינוּ חַסְדּוֹ, וֶאֱמֶת יְיָ לְעוֹלָם, הַלְלוּיָהּ:

הוֹדוּ לַיְיָ כִּי טוֹב,
כִּי לְעוֹלָם חַסְדּוֹ:

יֹאמַר נָא יִשְׂרָאֵל
כִּי לְעוֹלָם חַסְדּוֹ:

יֹאמְרוּ נָא בֵית אַהֲרֹן,
כִּי לְעוֹלָם חַסְדּוֹ:

יֹאמְרוּ נָא יִרְאֵי יְיָ,
כִּי לְעוֹלָם חַסְדּוֹ:

From the narrows I called upon the Lord; the Lord answered me by placing me in a great expanse. The Lord is with me; I have no fear of what man can do to me. The Lord is with me among my helpers; I shall see the defeat of my foes. It is better to seek refuge in the Lord than to trust in man. It is better to seek refuge in the Lord than to trust in princes. All nations have encompassed me; but in the name of the Lord, I routed them. They swarmed around me; but in the name of the Lord, I cut them down. They swarmed like bees about me, but they were extinguished like a fire of thorns; but in the name of the Lord, I cut them down. You pushed me that I might fall, but the Lord helped me. The Lord is my strength and song; He has become my salvation. The voice of rejoicing and salvation is heard in the tents of the righteous: "The right hand of the Lord does valiantly. The Lord's right hand is raised in triumph; the Lord's right hand does valiantly!" I shall not die, but live to relate the deeds of the Lord. The Lord has surely punished me, but He has not left me to die.

Open for me the gates of righteousness, that I may enter and praise the Lord. This is the gate of the Lord; the righteous may enter through it.

I thank Thee for Thou has answered me and have become my salvation. I thank Thee for Thou has answered me and have become my salvation.

The stone which the builders rejected has become the major cornerstone. The stone which the builders rejected has become the major cornerstone.

This the Lord's doing; It is marvelous in our eyes. This the Lord's doing; It is marvelous in our eyes.

This is the day which the Lord has made; We will be glad and rejoice on it. This is the day which the Lord has made; We will be glad and rejoice on it.

מִן הַמֵּצַר קָרָאתִי יָּהּ, עָנָנִי בַמֶּרְחָב יָהּ. יְיָ לִי לֹא אִירָא, מַה יַּעֲשֶׂה לִי אָדָם. יְיָ לִי בְּעֹזְרָי וַאֲנִי אֶרְאֶה בְשׂנְאָי. טוֹב לַחֲסוֹת בַּיְיָ מִבְּטֹחַ בָּאָדָם. טוֹב לַחֲסוֹת בַּיְיָ מִבְּטֹחַ בִּנְדִיבִים. כָּל גּוֹיִם סְבָבוּנִי, בְּשֵׁם יְיָ כִּי אֲמִילַם. סַבּוּנִי גַם סְבָבוּנִי, בְּשֵׁם יְיָ כִּי אֲמִילַם. סַבּוּנִי כִדְבֹרִים, דֹּעֲכוּ כְּאֵשׁ קוֹצִים, בְּשֵׁם יְיָ כִּי אֲמִילַם. דָּחֹה דְחִיתַנִי לִנְפֹּל, וַיְיָ עֲזָרָנִי. עָזִּי וְזִמְרָת יָהּ וַיְהִי לִי לִישׁוּעָה. קוֹל רִנָּה וִישׁוּעָה בְּאָהֳלֵי צַדִּיקִים, יְמִין יְיָ עֹשָׂה חָיִל. יְמִין יְיָ רוֹמֵמָה, יְמִין יְיָ עֹשָׂה חָיִל. לֹא אָמוּת כִּי אֶחְיֶה, וַאֲסַפֵּר מַעֲשֵׂי יָהּ. יַסֹּר יִסְּרַנִּי יָּהּ, וְלַמָּוֶת לֹא נְתָנָנִי.

פִּתְחוּ לִי שַׁעֲרֵי צֶדֶק, אָבֹא בָם, אוֹדֶה יָהּ. זֶה הַשַּׁעַר לַיְיָ, צַדִּיקִים יָבֹאוּ בוֹ.

אוֹדְךָ כִּי עֲנִיתָנִי וַתְּהִי לִי לִישׁוּעָה. אוֹדְךָ כִּי עֲנִיתָנִי וַתְּהִי לִי לִישׁוּעָה.

אֶבֶן מָאֲסוּ הַבּוֹנִים הָיְתָה לְרֹאשׁ פִּנָּה. אֶבֶן מָאֲסוּ הַבּוֹנִים הָיְתָה לְרֹאשׁ פִּנָּה.

מֵאֵת יְיָ הָיְתָה זֹּאת הִיא נִפְלָאת בְּעֵינֵינוּ. מֵאֵת יְיָ הָיְתָה זֹּאת הִיא נִפְלָאת בְּעֵינֵינוּ.

זֶה הַיּוֹם עָשָׂה יְיָ נָגִילָה וְנִשְׂמְחָה בוֹ. זֶה הַיּוֹם עָשָׂה יְיָ נָגִילָה וְנִשְׂמְחָה בוֹ.

O Lord, please save us!

O Lord, please save us!

O Lord, let us prosper!

O Lord, let us prosper!

Blessed be he who comes in the name of the Lord;
We bless you from the house of the Lord. Blessed be he who comes in the name of the Lord; We bless you from the house of the Lord.

The Lord is God who has shown us light; Bind the sacrifice with cords, up to the altar-horns. The Lord is God who has shown us light; Bind the sacrifice with cords, up to the altar-horns.

Thou art my God, and I thank Thee; Thou art my God, and I exalt Thee. Thou art my God, and I thank Thee; Thou art my God, and I exalt Thee.

Give thanks to the Lord, for He is good; His kindness endures forever. Give thanks to the Lord, for He is good; His kindness endures forever (Psalm 118:5-29).

Give thanks to the Lord, for He is good,
　　　　　　　　His kindness endures forever;
Give thanks to the God above gods,
　　　　　　　His kindness endures forever;
Give thanks to the Lord of lords,
　　　　　　　His kindness endures forever;
To Him who alone does great wonders,
　　　　　　　His kindness endures forever;
To Him who made the heavens with understanding,
　　　　　　　His kindness endures forever;
To Him who stretched the earth over the waters,
　　　　　　　His kindness endures forever;
To Him who made the great lights,
　　　　　　　His kindness endures forever;
The sun to reign by day,
　　　　　　　His kindness endures forever;
The moon and the stars to reign by night,
　　　　　　　His kindness endures forever;

אָנָּא יְיָ הוֹשִׁיעָה נָּא:
אָנָּא יְיָ הוֹשִׁיעָה נָּא:
אָנָּא יְיָ הַצְלִיחָה נָּא:
אָנָּא יְיָ הַצְלִיחָה נָּא:

בָּרוּךְ הַבָּא בְּשֵׁם יְיָ,
בֵּרַכְנוּכֶם מִבֵּית יְיָ.
בָּרוּךְ הַבָּא בְּשֵׁם יְיָ,
בֵּרַכְנוּכֶם מִבֵּית יְיָ.

אֵל יְיָ וַיָּאֶר לָנוּ. אִסְרוּ חַג בַּעֲבֹתִים
עַד קַרְנוֹת הַמִּזְבֵּחַ. אֵל יְיָ וַיָּאֶר לָנוּ.
אִסְרוּ חַג בַּעֲבֹתִים עַד קַרְנוֹת הַמִּזְבֵּחַ.

אֵלִי אַתָּה וְאוֹדֶךָּ, אֱלֹהַי אֲרוֹמְמֶךָּ.
אֵלִי אַתָּה וְאוֹדֶךָּ, אֱלֹהַי אֲרוֹמְמֶךָּ.

הוֹדוּ לַיְיָ כִּי טוֹב, כִּי לְעוֹלָם חַסְדּוֹ.
הוֹדוּ לַיְיָ כִּי טוֹב, כִּי לְעוֹלָם חַסְדּוֹ.

הוֹדוּ לַיְיָ כִּי טוֹב,
כִּי לְעוֹלָם חַסְדּוֹ:
הוֹדוּ לֵאלֹהֵי הָאֱלֹהִים,
כִּי לְעוֹלָם חַסְדּוֹ:
הוֹדוּ לַאֲדֹנֵי הָאֲדֹנִים,
כִּי לְעוֹלָם חַסְדּוֹ:
לְעֹשֵׂה נִפְלָאוֹת גְּדֹלוֹת לְבַדּוֹ,
כִּי לְעוֹלָם חַסְדּוֹ:
לְעֹשֵׂה הַשָּׁמַיִם בִּתְבוּנָה,
כִּי לְעוֹלָם חַסְדּוֹ:
לְרוֹקַע הָאָרֶץ עַל הַמָּיִם,
כִּי לְעוֹלָם חַסְדּוֹ:
לְעֹשֵׂה אוֹרִים גְּדֹלִים,
כִּי לְעוֹלָם חַסְדּוֹ:
אֶת הַשֶּׁמֶשׁ לְמֶמְשֶׁלֶת בַּיּוֹם,
כִּי לְעוֹלָם חַסְדּוֹ:
אֶת הַיָּרֵחַ וְכוֹכָבִים לְמֶמְשְׁלוֹת בַּלַּיְלָה,
כִּי לְעוֹלָם חַסְדּוֹ:

To Him who smote Egypt in their firstborn,	לְמַכֵּה מִצְרַיִם בִּבְכוֹרֵיהֶם,
His kindness endures forever;	כִּי לְעוֹלָם חַסְדּוֹ:
And took Israel out from among them,	וַיּוֹצֵא יִשְׂרָאֵל מִתּוֹכָם,
His kindness endures forever;	כִּי לְעוֹלָם חַסְדּוֹ:
With strong hand and outstretched arm,	בְּיָד חֲזָקָה וּבִזְרוֹעַ נְטוּיָה,
His kindness endures forever;	כִּי לְעוֹלָם חַסְדּוֹ:
To him who parted the Red Sea,	לְגֹזֵר יַם סוּף לִגְזָרִים,
His kindness endures forever;	כִּי לְעוֹלָם חַסְדּוֹ:
And caused Israel to pass through it,	וְהֶעֱבִיר יִשְׂרָאֵל בְּתוֹכוֹ,
His kindness endures forever;	כִּי לְעוֹלָם חַסְדּוֹ:
And threw Pharaoh and his host in the Red Sea,	וְנִעֵר פַּרְעֹה וְחֵילוֹ בְיַם סוּף,
His kindness endures forever;	כִּי לְעוֹלָם חַסְדּוֹ:
To Him who led His people through the wilderness,	לְמוֹלִיךְ עַמּוֹ בַּמִּדְבָּר,
His kindness endures forever;	כִּי לְעוֹלָם חַסְדּוֹ:
To Him who smote great kings,	לְמַכֵּה מְלָכִים גְּדֹלִים,
His kindness endures forever;	כִּי לְעוֹלָם חַסְדּוֹ:
And slew mighty kings,	וַיַּהֲרֹג מְלָכִים אַדִּירִים,
His kindness endures forever;	כִּי לְעוֹלָם חַסְדּוֹ:
Sihon, king of the Amorites,	לְסִיחוֹן מֶלֶךְ הָאֱמֹרִי,
His kindness endures forever;	כִּי לְעוֹלָם חַסְדּוֹ:
And Og, king of Bashan,	וּלְעוֹג מֶלֶךְ הַבָּשָׁן,
His kindness endures forever;	כִּי לְעוֹלָם חַסְדּוֹ:
And gave their land as an inheritance,	וְנָתַן אַרְצָם לְנַחֲלָה,
His kindness endures forever;	כִּי לְעוֹלָם חַסְדּוֹ:
An inheritance to Israel His servant,	נַחֲלָה לְיִשְׂרָאֵל עַבְדּוֹ,
His kindness endures forever;	כִּי לְעוֹלָם חַסְדּוֹ:
Who remembered us in our low state,	שֶׁבְּשִׁפְלֵנוּ זָכַר לָנוּ,
His kindness endures forever;	כִּי לְעוֹלָם חַסְדּוֹ:
And released us from our foes,	וַיִּפְרְקֵנוּ מִצָּרֵינוּ,
His kindness endures forever;	כִּי לְעוֹלָם חַסְדּוֹ:
Who gives food to all creatures,	נוֹתֵן לֶחֶם לְכָל בָּשָׂר,
His kindness endures forever;	כִּי לְעוֹלָם חַסְדּוֹ:
Give thanks to God of all heaven,	הוֹדוּ לְאֵל הַשָּׁמָיִם,
His kindness endures forever.	כִּי לְעוֹלָם חַסְדּוֹ:

The soul of every living being shall bless thy name,
Lord our God the spirit of all flesh shall ever glorify
and exalt thy remembrance, our King. Throughout
eternity Thou art God. Besides Thee we have no king
who redeems and saves, ransoms and rescues, sustains
and shows mercy in all times of trouble and distress.
We have no King but Thee-God of the first and of the
last, God of all creatures, Master of all generations,
One acclaimed with a multitude of praises, He who
guides His world with kindness and His creatures with
mercy. The Lord neither slumbers nor sleeps; He rouses
those who sleep and wakens those who slumber; He
enables the speechless to speak and loosens the bonds
of the captives; He supports those who are fallen and
raises those who are bowed down. To Thee alone we
give thanks. Were our mouth filled with song as the
ocean, and our tongue with joy as the endless waves;
were our lips full of praise as the wide heavens, and
our eyes shining like the sun or the moon; were our
hands spread out in prayer as the eagles of the sky and
our feet running as swiftly as the deer-we should still
be unable to thank Thee and bless thy name, Lord our
God and God of our fathers, for one of the thousands
and even myriads of favors which Thou hast bestowed
on our fathers and on us. Thou hast liberated us from
Egypt, Lord our God, and redeemed us from the house
of slavery. Thou has fed us in famine and sustained us
with plenty. Thou hast saved us from the sword, helped
us to escape the plague, and spared us from severe and
enduring diseases. Until now Thy mercy has helped us,
and Thy kindness has not forsaken us; mayest Thou,
Lord our God, never abandon us. Therefore, the limbs
which Thou has given us, the spirit and soul which
Thou has breathed into our nostrils, and the tongue
which Thou hast placed in our mouth, shall all thank
and bless, praise and glorify, exalt and revere, sanctify
and acclaim thy name, our King. To Thee, every mouth
shall offer thanks; every tongue shall vow allegiance;

נִשְׁמַת כָּל חַי תְּבָרֵךְ אֶת שִׁמְךָ יְיָ
אֱלֹהֵינוּ, וְרוּחַ כָּל בָּשָׂר תְּפָאֵר וּתְרוֹמֵם
זִכְרְךָ מַלְכֵּנוּ תָּמִיד. מִן הָעוֹלָם וְעַד
הָעוֹלָם אַתָּה אֵל, וּמִבַּלְעָדֶיךָ אֵין לָנוּ
מֶלֶךְ גּוֹאֵל וּמוֹשִׁיעַ, פּוֹדֶה וּמַצִּיל
וּמְפַרְנֵס וּמְרַחֵם בְּכָל עֵת צָרָה וְצוּקָה.
אֵין לָנוּ מֶלֶךְ אֶלָּא אָתָּה. אֱלֹהֵי
הָרִאשׁוֹנִים וְהָאַחֲרוֹנִים, אֱלֹהַּ כָּל
בְּרִיּוֹת, אֲדוֹן כָּל תּוֹלָדוֹת, הַמְהֻלָּל
בְּרֹב הַתִּשְׁבָּחוֹת, הַמְנַהֵג עוֹלָמוֹ
בְּחֶסֶד וּבְרִיּוֹתָיו בְּרַחֲמִים. וַיְיָ לֹא יָנוּם
וְלֹא יִישָׁן, הַמְעוֹרֵר יְשֵׁנִים וְהַמֵּקִיץ
נִרְדָּמִים, וְהַמֵּשִׂיחַ אִלְּמִים וְהַמַּתִּיר
אֲסוּרִים, וְהַסּוֹמֵךְ נוֹפְלִים וְהַזּוֹקֵף
כְּפוּפִים, לְךָ לְבַדְּךָ אֲנַחְנוּ מוֹדִים.
אִלּוּ פִינוּ מָלֵא שִׁירָה כַּיָּם, וּלְשׁוֹנֵנוּ
רִנָּה כַּהֲמוֹן גַּלָּיו, וְשִׂפְתוֹתֵינוּ שֶׁבַח
כְּמֶרְחֲבֵי רָקִיעַ, וְעֵינֵינוּ מְאִירוֹת
כַּשֶּׁמֶשׁ וְכַיָּרֵחַ, וְיָדֵינוּ פְרוּשׂוֹת
כְּנִשְׁרֵי שָׁמַיִם, וְרַגְלֵינוּ קַלּוֹת כָּאַיָּלוֹת,
אֵין אֲנַחְנוּ מַסְפִּיקִים לְהוֹדוֹת
לְךָ, יְיָ אֱלֹהֵינוּ וֵאלֹהֵי אֲבוֹתֵינוּ,
וּלְבָרֵךְ אֶת שְׁמֶךָ, עַל אַחַת מֵאֶלֶף
אַלְפֵי אֲלָפִים וְרִבֵּי רְבָבוֹת פְּעָמִים
הַטּוֹבוֹת שֶׁעָשִׂיתָ עִם אֲבוֹתֵינוּ
וְעִמָּנוּ. מִמִּצְרַיִם גְּאַלְתָּנוּ, יְיָ אֱלֹהֵינוּ,
וּמִבֵּית עֲבָדִים פְּדִיתָנוּ, בְּרָעָב זַנְתָּנוּ
וּבְשָׂבָע כִּלְכַּלְתָּנוּ, מֵחֶרֶב הִצַּלְתָּנוּ
וּמִדֶּבֶר מִלַּטְתָּנוּ, וּמֵחֳלָיִם רָעִים
וְרַבִּים וְנֶאֱמָנִים דִּלִּיתָנוּ. עַד הֵנָּה
עֲזָרוּנוּ רַחֲמֶיךָ וְלֹא עֲזָבוּנוּ חֲסָדֶיךָ,
וְאַל תִּטְּשֵׁנוּ יְיָ אֱלֹהֵינוּ לָנֶצַח. עַל כֵּן
אֵבָרִים שֶׁפִּלַּגְתָּ בָּנוּ וְרוּחַ וּנְשָׁמָה
שֶׁנָּפַחְתָּ בְּאַפֵּינוּ וְלָשׁוֹן אֲשֶׁר שַׂמְתָּ
בְּפִינוּ, הֵן הֵם יוֹדוּ וִיבָרְכוּ וִישַׁבְּחוּ
וִיפָאֲרוּ וִירוֹמְמוּ וְיַעֲרִיצוּ וְיַקְדִּישׁוּ
וְיַמְלִיכוּ אֶת שִׁמְךָ מַלְכֵּנוּ. כִּי כָל פֶּה
לְךָ יוֹדֶה, וְכָל לָשׁוֹן לְךָ תִשָּׁבַע, וְכָל

every knee shall bend, and all who stand erect shall bow.
All hearts shall revere Thee, and men's inner beings shall
sing to thy name, as it is written: "all my bones shall say: O
Lord, who is like Thee? Thou savest the poor man from one
that is stronger, the poor and needy from one who would rob
him." Who may be likened to Thee? Who is equal to Thee?
Who can be compared to Thee? O Great, mighty and revered
God, supreme God is the Master of heaven and earth. Let us
praise, acclaim and glorify Thee and bless thy holy name, as
it is said: "A Psalm of David: Bless the Lord, O my soul, and
let my whole inner being bless His holy name."

O God in thy mighty acts of power, great in the honor
of thy name, powerful forever and revered for thy awe-
inspiring acts, O King seated upon a high and lofty throne!
He who abidest forever, exalted and holy is His name. And it
is written: "Rejoice in the Lord, you righteous; it is pleasant
for the upright to give praise."
By the mouth of the upright you shall be praised;
By the words of the righteous you shall be blessed;
By the tongue of the pious you shall be exalted;
And in the midst of the holy you shall be sanctified.

In the assemblies of the multitudes of
thy people, the house of Israel, with song
shall thy name, our King, be glorified in every
generation. For it is the duty of all creatures
to thank, praise, laud, extol, exalt, adore,
and bless Thee; even beyond the songs and
praises of David the son of Jesse, thy anointed
servant.

Praise be thy name forever, our King, who
rules and is great and holy in heaven and on earth; for to
Thee, Lord our God, it is fitting to render song and praise,
hallel and psalms, power and dominion, victory, glory
and might, praise and beauty, holiness and sovereignty,
blessings and thanks, from now and forever.

בֶּרֶךְ לְךָ תִכְרַע, וְכָל קוֹמָה לְפָנֶיךָ
תִשְׁתַּחֲוֶה, וְכָל לְבָבוֹת יִירָאוּךָ, וְכָל
קֶרֶב וּכְלָיוֹת יְזַמְּרוּ לִשְׁמֶךָ, כַּדָּבָר
שֶׁכָּתוּב, כָּל עַצְמֹתַי תֹּאמַרְנָה: יְיָ, מִי
כָמוֹךָ!, מַצִּיל עָנִי מֵחָזָק מִמֶּנּוּ וְעָנִי
וְאֶבְיוֹן מִגֹּזְלוֹ. מִי יִדְמֶה לָּךְ וּמִי יִשְׁוֶה
לָּךְ וּמִי יַעֲרָךְ לָךְ, הָאֵל הַגָּדוֹל, הַגִּבּוֹר
וְהַנּוֹרָא, אֵל עֶלְיוֹן, קֹנֵה שָׁמַיִם וָאָרֶץ.
נְהַלֶּלְךָ וּנְשַׁבֵּחֲךָ וּנְפָאֶרְךָ וּנְבָרֵךְ אֶת
שֵׁם קָדְשֶׁךָ, כָּאָמוּר: לְדָוִד, בָּרְכִי נַפְשִׁי
אֶת יְיָ וְכָל קְרָבַי אֶת שֵׁם קָדְשׁוֹ.

הָאֵל בְּתַעֲצֻמוֹת עֻזֶּךָ, הַגָּדוֹל
בִּכְבוֹד שְׁמֶךָ, הַגִּבּוֹר לָנֶצַח וְהַנּוֹרָא
בְּנוֹרְאוֹתֶיךָ, הַמֶּלֶךְ הַיּוֹשֵׁב עַל כִּסֵּא רָם
וְנִשָּׂא. שׁוֹכֵן עַד מָרוֹם וְקָדוֹשׁ שְׁמוֹ.
וְכָתוּב: רַנְּנוּ צַדִּיקִים בַּיְיָ, לַיְשָׁרִים
נָאוָה תְהִלָּה.
בְּפִי יְשָׁרִים תִּתְהַלָּל
וּבְדִבְרֵי צַדִּיקִים תִּתְבָּרַךְ
וּבִלְשׁוֹן חֲסִידִים תִּתְרוֹמָם
וּבְקֶרֶב קְדוֹשִׁים תִּתְקַדָּשׁ

וּבְמַקְהֲלוֹת רִבְבוֹת עַמְּךָ בֵּית יִשְׂרָאֵל
בְּרִנָּה יִתְפָּאֵר שִׁמְךָ, מַלְכֵּנוּ, בְּכָל דּוֹר
וָדוֹר. שֶׁכֵּן חוֹבַת כָּל הַיְצוּרִים, לְפָנֶיךָ
יְיָ אֱלֹהֵינוּ וֵאלֹהֵי אֲבוֹתֵינוּ לְהוֹדוֹת,
לְהַלֵּל, לְשַׁבֵּחַ, לְפָאֵר, לְרוֹמֵם, לְהַדֵּר,
לְבָרֵךְ, לְעַלֵּה וּלְקַלֵּס עַל כָּל דִּבְרֵי
שִׁירוֹת וְתִשְׁבְּחוֹת דָּוִד בֶּן יִשַׁי עַבְדְּךָ,
מְשִׁיחֶךָ.

יִשְׁתַּבַּח שִׁמְךָ לָעַד מַלְכֵּנוּ, הָאֵל הַמֶּלֶךְ
הַגָּדוֹל וְהַקָּדוֹשׁ בַּשָּׁמַיִם וּבָאָרֶץ, כִּי לְךָ נָאֶה,
יְיָ אֱלֹהֵינוּ וֵאלֹהֵי אֲבוֹתֵינוּ, שִׁיר וּשְׁבָחָה, הַלֵּל
וְזִמְרָה, עֹז וּמֶמְשָׁלָה, נֶצַח, גְּדֻלָּה וּגְבוּרָה,
תְּהִלָּה וְתִפְאֶרֶת, קְדֻשָׁה וּמַלְכוּת, בְּרָכוֹת
וְהוֹדָאוֹת מֵעַתָּה וְעַד עוֹלָם.

All thy works praise Thee, Lord our God; thy pious followers who perform thy will, and all thy people the house of Israel, praise, thank, bless, glorify, extol, exalt, revere, sanctify, and coronate thy name, our King. To Thee it is fitting to give thanks, and unto thy name it is proper to sing praises, for Thou art God eternal.

יְהַלְלוּךָ יי אֱלֹהֵינוּ כָּל מַעֲשֶׂיךָ, וַחֲסִידֶיךָ צַדִּיקִים עוֹשֵׂי רְצוֹנֶךָ, וְכָל עַמְּךָ בֵּית יִשְׂרָאֵל בְּרִנָּה יוֹדוּ וִיבָרְכוּ, וִישַׁבְּחוּ וִיפָאֲרוּ, וִירוֹמְמוּ וְיַעֲרִיצוּ, וְיַקְדִּישׁוּ וְיַמְלִיכוּ אֶת שִׁמְךָ, מַלְכֵּנוּ. כִּי לְךָ טוֹב לְהוֹדוֹת וּלְשִׁמְךָ נָאֶה לְזַמֵּר, כִּי מֵעוֹלָם וְעַד עוֹלָם אַתָּה אֵל. בָּרוּךְ אַתָּה יְיָ, מֶלֶךְ מְהֻלָּל בַּתִּשְׁבָּחוֹת.

The Fourth Cup

Over the Fourth cup of wine, we recite:

Blessed art Thou, Lord our God, King of the universe, who createst the fruit of the vine.

בָּרוּךְ אַתָּה יְיָ אֱלֹהֵינוּ מֶלֶךְ הָעוֹלָם בּוֹרֵא פְּרִי הַגָּפֶן.

We drink the fourth cup of wine while reclining, then say:

Blessed, art Thou, Lord our God, King of the universe, for the vine and its fruit, and for the produce of the field, for the beautiful and spacious land which Thou gave to our fathers as a heritage to eat of its fruit and to enjoy its goodness. Have mercy, Lord our God, on Israel thy people, on Jerusalem thy city, on Zion the abode of thy glory, on thy altar and thy Temple. Rebuild Jerusalem, the holy city, speedily in our days. Bring us there and cheer us with its restoration; may we eat of its fruit and enjoy of its goodness; may we bless Thee for it in holiness and purity. [Favor us and strengthen us on this Sabbath day] and grant us happiness on this Feast of Matzot; For Thou, O Lord, are good and beneficent to all, and we thank Thee for the land and the fruit of the vine. Blessed art Thou, O Lord for the land and the fruit of the vine.

בָּרוּךְ אַתָּה יְיָ אֱלֹהֵינוּ מֶלֶךְ הָעוֹלָם, עַל הַגֶּפֶן וְעַל פְּרִי הַגֶּפֶן, וְעַל תְּנוּבַת הַשָּׂדֶה, וְעַל אֶרֶץ חֶמְדָּה טוֹבָה וּרְחָבָה שֶׁרָצִיתָ וְהִנְחַלְתָּ לַאֲבוֹתֵינוּ לֶאֱכֹל מִפִּרְיָהּ וְלִשְׂבֹּעַ מִטּוּבָהּ. רַחֵם נָא יְיָ אֱלֹהֵינוּ עַל יִשְׂרָאֵל עַמֶּךָ וְעַל יְרוּשָׁלַיִם עִירֶךָ וְעַל צִיּוֹן מִשְׁכַּן כְּבוֹדֶךָ וְעַל מִזְבַּחֶךָ וְעַל הֵיכָלֶךָ, וּבְנֵה יְרוּשָׁלַיִם עִיר הַקֹּדֶשׁ בִּמְהֵרָה בְיָמֵינוּ, וְהַעֲלֵנוּ לְתוֹכָהּ וְשַׂמְּחֵנוּ בְּבִנְיָנָהּ וְנֹאכַל מִפִּרְיָהּ וְנִשְׂבַּע מִטּוּבָהּ וּנְבָרֶכְךָ עָלֶיהָ בִּקְדֻשָּׁה וּבְטָהֳרָה. [בְּשַׁבָּת: וּרְצֵה וְהַחֲלִיצֵנוּ בְּיוֹם הַשַּׁבָּת הַזֶּה] וְשַׂמְּחֵנוּ בְּיוֹם חַג הַמַּצּוֹת הַזֶּה. כִּי אַתָּה יְיָ טוֹב וּמֵיטִיב לַכֹּל, וְנוֹדֶה לְךָ עַל הָאָרֶץ וְעַל פְּרִי הַגָּפֶן. בָּרוּךְ אַתָּה יְיָ, עַל הָאָרֶץ וְעַל פְּרִי הַגָּפֶן.

Nirtzah

The Seder now concludes
according to Halacha, Complete
in all laws and ordinances.
Just as we were privileged to
arrange it tonight, So may we
be granted to perform it again.
O Pure One who dwellest in
the heights above, Establish
us as a countless people once
again, Speedily guide thy plants
Israel as a redeemed people, To
the land of Zion with song.

Next year in Jerusalem!

נִרְצָה

חֲסַל סִדּוּר פֶּסַח כְּהִלְכָתוֹ,

כְּכָל מִשְׁפָּטוֹ וְחֻקָּתוֹ.

כַּאֲשֶׁר זָכִינוּ לְסַדֵּר אוֹתוֹ,

כֵּן נִזְכֶּה לַעֲשׂוֹתוֹ.

זָךְ שׁוֹכֵן מְעוֹנָה,

קוֹמֵם קְהַל עֲדַת מִי מָנָה.

בְּקָרוֹב נַהֵל נִטְעֵי כַנָּה,

פְּדוּיִם לְצִיּוֹן בְּרִנָּה.

לְשָׁנָה הַבָּאָה בִּירוּשָׁלָיִם!

On the first night, recite:

וּבְכֵן "וַיְהִי בַּחֲצִי הַלַּיְלָה".

It came to pass at midnight. ───────────────

Thou didst perform most wonders **at night**, In the early watches of **this night**. The righteous convert Abraham didst Thou cause to triumph **at night**.

It came to pass at midnight.

אָז רוֹב נִסִּים הִפְלֵאתָ בַּ**לַּיְלָה**,
בְּרֹאשׁ אַשְׁמוּרוֹת זֶה **הַלַּיְלָה**,
גֵּר צֶדֶק נִצַּחְתּוֹ כְּנֶחֱלַק לוֹ **לַיְלָה**,
וַיְהִי בַּחֲצִי הַלַּיְלָה.

Grar's king Abimelech, didst Thou judge in a dream **by night**. Thou didst frighten Laban in the dark **of night**. Israel overcame an angel and won **by night**.

It came to pass at midnight.

דַּנְתָּ מֶלֶךְ גְּרָר בַּחֲלוֹם **הַלַּיְלָה**,
הִפְחַדְתָּ אֲרַמִּי בְּאֶמֶשׁ **לַיְלָה**,
וַיָּשַׂר יִשְׂרָאֵל לְמַלְאָךְ וַיּוּכַל לוֹ **לַיְלָה**,
וַיְהִי בַּחֲצִי הַלַּיְלָה.

Egypt's firstborn didst Thou crush at **midnight.** Their strength they found not when they rose **at night**. Sisera, prince of Harashet, didst Thou rout through stars of the **night**.

It came to pass at midnight.

זֶרַע בְּכוֹרֵי פַתְרוֹס מָחַצְתָּ בַּחֲצִי **הַלַּיְלָה**,
חֵילָם לֹא מָצְאוּ בְּקוּמָם בַּ**לַּיְלָה**,
טִיסַת נְגִיד חֲרֹשֶׁת סִלִּיתָ בְכוֹכְבֵי **לַיְלָה**,
וַיְהִי בַּחֲצִי הַלַּיְלָה.

Senncherib, the blasphemer, didst Thou disgrace **by night**. Babylon's idol fell in the dark **of night**. Daniel was shown the secret of the king's dream of the **night**.

It came to pass at midnight.

יָעַץ מְחָרֵף לְנוֹפֵף אִוּוּי, הוֹבַשְׁתָּ פְגָרָיו בַּ**לַּיְלָה**,
כָּרַע בֵּל וּמַצָּבוֹ בְּאִישׁוֹן **לַיְלָה**,
לְאִישׁ חֲמוּדוֹת נִגְלָה רָז חֲזוֹת **לַיְלָה**,
וַיְהִי בַּחֲצִי הַלַּיְלָה.

Belshazzar, who drank from the Temple's vessel, was killed **that same night**. Daniel who was saved from the lion's den interpreted the visions **of night**. Hateful Haman the Agagite wrote letters in the **night**.

It came to pass at midnight.

מִשְׁתַּכֵּר בִּכְלֵי קֹדֶשׁ נֶהֱרַג בּוֹ בַּ**לַּיְלָה**,
נוֹשַׁע מִבּוֹר אֲרָיוֹת פּוֹתֵר בְּעִתּוּתֵי **לַיְלָה**,
שִׂנְאָה נָטַר אֲגָגִי וְכָתַב סְפָרִים **לַיְלָה**,
וַיְהִי בַּחֲצִי הַלַּיְלָה.

Thou didst triumph against Haman in the king's sleepless **night**. Trample the winepress and aid those who ask. "What of **the night**?" The watchman responds: "Morning comes **after night**".

It came to pass at midnight.

עוֹרַרְתָּ נִצְחֲךָ עָלָיו בְּנֶדֶד שְׁנַת **לַיְלָה**,
פּוּרָה תִדְרוֹךְ לְשׁוֹמֵר מַה **מִּלַּיְלָה**,
צָרַח כַּשּׁוֹמֵר וְשָׂח אָתָא בֹקֶר וְגַם **לַיְלָה**,
וַיְהִי בַּחֲצִי הַלַּיְלָה.

Hasten the eternal day which is not really day or **night**. Exalted One, proclaim that Thine are day and **night**. Set guards about thy city all day and **night**. Brighten as day the darkness of the **night**.

It came to pass at midnight.

קָרֵב יוֹם אֲשֶׁר הוּא לֹא יוֹם וְלֹא **לַיְלָה**,
רָם הוֹדַע כִּי לְךָ הַיּוֹם אַף לְךָ **הַלַּיְלָה**,
שׁוֹמְרִים הַפְקֵד לְעִירְךָ כָּל הַיּוֹם וְכָל **הַלַּיְלָה**,
תָּאִיר כְּאוֹר יוֹם חֶשְׁכַת **לַיְלָה**,
וַיְהִי בַּחֲצִי הַלַּיְלָה:

And you shall say: It is the Pesach sacrifice. _____ **וּבְכֵן וַאֲמַרְתֶּם זֶבַח פֶּסַח.**

Thy wondrous powers didst Thou display **on Pesach**; Chief of all feasts didst Thou make **Pesach**; Thou didst reveal Thyself to Abraham on the midnight **of Pesach**;

And you shall say: It is the Pesach sacrifice.

אֹמֶץ גְּבוּרוֹתֶיךָ הִפְלֵאתָ **בַּפֶּסַח**,
בְּרֹאשׁ כָּל מוֹעֲדוֹת נִשֵּׂאתָ **פֶּסַח**,
גִּלִּיתָ לָאֶזְרָחִי חֲצוֹת לֵיל **פֶּסַח**,
וַאֲמַרְתֶּם זֶבַח פֶּסַח.

To his door didst Thou come at noon **on Pesach**; With matzot he served angels **on Pesach**; To the herd he ran for the ox recalling Joseph **on Pesach**;

And you shall say: It is the Pesach sacrifice.

דְּלָתָיו דָּפַקְתָּ כְּחֹם הַיּוֹם **בַּפֶּסַח**,
הִסְעִיד נוֹצְצִים עֻגוֹת מַצּוֹת **בַּפֶּסַח**,
וְאֶל הַבָּקָר רָץ זֵכֶר לְשׁוֹר עֵרֶךְ **פֶּסַח**,
וַאֲמַרְתֶּם זֶבַח פֶּסַח.

The men of Sodom were burned in wrath **on Pesach**; Lot was saved, he baked matzot at the end **of Pesach**; Thou didst sweep and destroy Egypt when passing **on Pesach**;

And you shall say: It is the Pesach sacrifice.

זֹעֲמוּ סְדוֹמִים וְלֹהֲטוּ בָּאֵשׁ **בַּפֶּסַח**,
חֻלַּץ לוֹט מֵהֶם, וּמַצּוֹת אָפָה בְּקֵץ **פֶּסַח**,
טִאטֵאתָ אַדְמַת מֹף וְנֹף בְּעָבְרְךָ **בַּפֶּסַח**,
וַאֲמַרְתֶּם זֶבַח פֶּסַח.

Lord, every Egyptian firstborn Thou didst crush **on Pesach**; But thy firstborn Thou didst passover on the **Pesach**; So that no evil destroyed Israel's homes **on Pesach**;

And you shall say: It is the Pesach sacrifice.

יָהּ, רֹאשׁ כָּל אוֹן מָחַצְתָּ בְּלֵיל שִׁמּוּר **פֶּסַח**,
כַּבִּיר, עַל בֵּן בְּכוֹר פָּסַחְתָּ בְּדַם **פֶּסַח**,
לְבִלְתִּי תֵת מַשְׁחִית לָבֹא בִּפְתָחַי **בַּפֶּסַח**,
וַאֲמַרְתֶּם זֶבַח פֶּסַח.

The well-locked city of Jericho fell **on Pesach**; Midian was destroyed through a barley-cake from the Omer **of Pesach**; Assyria's mighty armies were consumed by fire **on Pesach**;

And you shall say: It is the Pesach sacrifice.

מְסֻגֶּרֶת סֻגְּרָה בְּעִתּוֹתֵי **פֶּסַח**,
נִשְׁמְדָה מִדְיָן בִּצְלִיל שְׂעוֹרֵי עֹמֶר **פֶּסַח**,
שֹׂרְפוּ מִשְׁמַנֵּי פּוּל וְלוּד בִּיקַד יְקוֹד **פֶּסַח**,
וַאֲמַרְתֶּם זֶבַח פֶּסַח.

Senncherib would have held his ground at Nov but the siege **on Pesach**; A hand inscribed Babylon's fate **on Pesach**; Babylon's festive table was destroyed **on Pesach**;

And you shall say: It is the Pesach sacrifice.

עוֹד הַיּוֹם בְּנֹב לַעֲמוֹד, עַד גָּעָה עוֹנַת **פֶּסַח**,
פַּס יָד כָּתְבָה לְקַעֲקֵעַ צוּל **בַּפֶּסַח**,
צָפֹה הַצָּפִית עָרוֹךְ הַשֻּׁלְחָן, **בַּפֶּסַח**,
וַאֲמַרְתֶּם זֶבַח פֶּסַח.

Esther called a three-day fast **on Pesach**; Thou didst hang the evil Haman **on Pesach**; Doubly, wilt Thou punish Edom **on Pesach**; Let Thy mighty arm save us from harm on the night **of Pesach**;

And you shall say: It is the Pesach sacrifice.

קָהָל כִּנְּסָה הֲדַסָּה צוֹם לְשַׁלֵּשׁ **בַּפֶּסַח**,
רֹאשׁ מִבֵּית רָשָׁע מָחַצְתָּ בְּעֵץ חֲמִשִּׁים **בַּפֶּסַח**,
שְׁתֵּי אֵלֶּה רֶגַע, תָּבִיא לְעוּצִית **בַּפֶּסַח**,
תָּעֹז יָדְךָ וְתָרוּם יְמִינֶךָ, כְּלֵיל הִתְקַדֶּשׁ חַג **פֶּסַח**,
וַאֲמַרְתֶּם זֶבַח פֶּסַח.

Beautiful praises are His due. ──────────────────── כִּי לוֹ נָאֶה, כִּי לוֹ יָאֶה.

Powerful in kingship, truly chosen, His troops sing to Him: "Thine only Thine, O Lord, is the Majestic Kingdom."
Beautiful praises are His due.

אַדִּיר בִּמְלוּכָה, **בָּ**חוּר כַּהֲלָכָה,
גְּדוּדָיו יאמְרוּ לוֹ:
לְךָ וּלְךָ, לְךָ כִּי לְךָ, לְךָ אַף לְךָ, לְךָ יְיָ הַמַּמְלָכָה.
כִּי לוֹ נָאֶה, כִּי לוֹ יָאֶה.

Famous in kingship, truly glorious, His faithful sing to Him: "Thine only Thine, O Lord, is the Majestic Kingdom."
Beautiful praises are His due.

דָּגוּל בִּמְלוּכָה, **הָ**דוּר כַּהֲלָכָה,
וָתִיקָיו יאמְרוּ לוֹ:
לְךָ וּלְךָ, לְךָ כִּי לְךָ, לְךָ אַף לְךָ, לְךָ יְיָ הַמַּמְלָכָה.
כִּי לוֹ נָאֶה, כִּי לוֹ יָאֶה.

Guiltless in kingship, truly strong, His angels sing to Him: "Thine only Thine, O Lord, is the Majestic Kingdom."
Beautiful praises are His due.

זַכַּאי בִּמְלוּכָה, **חָ**סִין כַּהֲלָכָה,
טַפְסְרָיו יאמְרוּ לוֹ:
לְךָ וּלְךָ, לְךָ כִּי לְךָ, לְךָ אַף לְךָ, לְךָ יְיָ הַמַּמְלָכָה.
כִּי לוֹ נָאֶה, כִּי לוֹ יָאֶה.

Alone in kingship, truly powerful, His scholars sing to Him: "Thine only Thine, O Lord, is the Majestic Kingdom."
Beautiful praises are His due.

יָחִיד בִּמְלוּכָה, **כַּ**בִּיר כַּהֲלָכָה,
לְמוּדָיו יאמְרוּ לוֹ:
לְךָ וּלְךָ, לְךָ כִּי לְךָ, לְךָ אַף לְךָ, לְךָ יְיָ הַמַּמְלָכָה.
כִּי לוֹ נָאֶה, כִּי לוֹ יָאֶה.

Commanding in kingship, truly revered, His near ones sing to Him: "Thine only Thine, O Lord, is the Majestic Kingdom."
Beautiful praises are His due.

מוֹשֵׁל בִּמְלוּכָה, **נ**וֹרָא כַּהֲלָכָה,
סְבִיבָיו יאמְרוּ לוֹ:
לְךָ וּלְךָ, לְךָ כִּי לְךָ, לְךָ אַף לְךָ, לְךָ יְיָ הַמַּמְלָכָה.
כִּי לוֹ נָאֶה, כִּי לוֹ יָאֶה.

Humble in kingship, truly redeeming, His righteous sing to Him: "Thine only Thine, O Lord, is the Majestic Kingdom."
Beautiful praises are His due.

עָנָו בִּמְלוּכָה, **פּ**וֹדֶה כַּהֲלָכָה,
צַדִּיקָיו יאמְרוּ לוֹ:
לְךָ וּלְךָ, לְךָ כִּי לְךָ, לְךָ אַף לְךָ, לְךָ יְיָ הַמַּמְלָכָה.
כִּי לוֹ נָאֶה, כִּי לוֹ יָאֶה.

Holy in kingship, truly merciful, His angels sing to Him: "Thine only Thine, O Lord, is the Majestic Kingdom."
Beautiful praises are His due.

קָדוֹשׁ בִּמְלוּכָה, **רַ**חוּם כַּהֲלָכָה,
שִׁנְאַנָּיו יאמְרוּ לוֹ:
לְךָ וּלְךָ, לְךָ כִּי לְךָ, לְךָ אַף לְךָ, לְךָ יְיָ הַמַּמְלָכָה.
כִּי לוֹ נָאֶה, כִּי לוֹ יָאֶה.

Indomitable in kingship, truly sustaining, His innocent sing to Him: "Thine only Thine, O Lord, is the Majestic Kingdom."
Beautiful praises are His due.

תַּקִּיף בִּמְלוּכָה, **תּ**וֹמֵךְ כַּהֲלָכָה,
תְּמִימָיו יאמְרוּ לוֹ:
לְךָ וּלְךָ, לְךָ כִּי לְךָ, לְךָ אַף לְךָ, לְךָ יְיָ הַמַּמְלָכָה.
כִּי לוֹ נָאֶה, כִּי לוֹ יָאֶה.

May He build His temple very soon.	יִבְנֶה בֵיתוֹ בְּקָרוֹב,
O God, build thy temple speedily.	**בִּמְהֵרָה בִּמְהֵרָה, בְּיָמֵינוּ בְּקָרוֹב.**
	אֵל בְּנֵה, בְּנֵה בֵיתְךָ בְּקָרוֹב.
He is chosen, great, and famous;	בָּחוּר הוּא, גָּדוֹל הוּא, דָּגוּל הוּא,
May He build His temple very soon.	יִבְנֶה בֵיתוֹ בְּקָרוֹב,
O God, build thy temple speedily.	**בִּמְהֵרָה בִּמְהֵרָה, בְּיָמֵינוּ בְּקָרוֹב.**
	אֵל בְּנֵה, בְּנֵה בֵיתְךָ בְּקָרוֹב.
He is glorious, pure and guiltless;	הָדוּר הוּא, וָתִיק הוּא, זַכַּאי הוּא,
May He build His temple very soon.	חָסִיד הוּא,
O God, build thy temple speedily.	יִבְנֶה בֵיתוֹ בְּקָרוֹב,
He is pious, clean and unique;	**בִּמְהֵרָה בִּמְהֵרָה, בְּיָמֵינוּ בְּקָרוֹב.**
May He build His temple very soon.	**אֵל בְּנֵה, בְּנֵה בֵיתְךָ בְּקָרוֹב.**
O God, build thy temple speedily.	טָהוֹר הוּא, יָחִיד הוּא, כַּבִּיר הוּא,
He is powerful, wise and majestic;	לָמוּד הוּא, מֶלֶךְ הוּא, נוֹרָא הוּא,
May He build His temple very soon.	סַגִּיב הוּא, עִזּוּז הוּא, פּוֹדֶה הוּא,
O God, build thy temple speedily.	צַדִּיק הוּא,
He is revered, eminent and strong;	יִבְנֶה בֵיתוֹ בְּקָרוֹב,
May He build His temple very soon.	**בִּמְהֵרָה בִּמְהֵרָה, בְּיָמֵינוּ בְּקָרוֹב.**
O God, build thy temple speedily.	**אֵל בְּנֵה, בְּנֵה בֵיתְךָ בְּקָרוֹב.**
He is redeeming, righteous and holy;	קָדוֹשׁ הוּא, רַחוּם הוּא, שַׁדַּי הוּא,
May He build His temple very soon.	תַּקִּיף הוּא,
O God, build thy temple speedily.	יִבְנֶה בֵיתוֹ בְּקָרוֹב,
He is merciful, ominipotent, and indomitable;	**בִּמְהֵרָה בִּמְהֵרָה, בְּיָמֵינוּ בְּקָרוֹב.**
May He build His temple very soon.	**אֵל בְּנֵה, בְּנֵה בֵיתְךָ בְּקָרוֹב.**
O God, build thy temple speedily.	

On the second night of Passover, we begin the counting of the Omer:

Blessed are you, Lord our God, King of the Universe, who has sanctified us with the commandments and commanded us to count the Omer.	בָּרוּךְ אַתָּה יְיָ אֱלֹהֵינוּ מֶלֶךְ הָעוֹלָם אֲשֶׁר קִדְּשָׁנוּ בְּמִצְוֹתָיו וְצִוָּנוּ עַל סְפִירַת הָעֹמֶר.
Today is day one of the Omer.	**הַיּוֹם יוֹם אֶחָד לָעֹמֶר.**

אֶחָד מִי יוֹדֵעַ?

אֶחָד אֲנִי יוֹדֵעַ:
אֶחָד אֱלֹהֵינוּ שֶׁבַּשָּׁמַיִם וּבָאָרֶץ.

שְׁנַיִם מִי יוֹדֵעַ?

שְׁנַיִם אֲנִי יוֹדֵעַ: שְׁנֵי לֻחוֹת הַבְּרִית,
אֶחָד אֱלֹהֵינוּ שֶׁבַּשָּׁמַיִם וּבָאָרֶץ.

שְׁלֹשָׁה מִי יוֹדֵעַ?

שְׁלֹשָׁה אֲנִי יוֹדֵעַ: שְׁלֹשָׁה אָבוֹת,
שְׁנֵי לֻחוֹת הַבְּרִית,
אֶחָד אֱלֹהֵינוּ שֶׁבַּשָּׁמַיִם וּבָאָרֶץ.

אַרְבַּע מִי יוֹדֵעַ?

אַרְבַּע אֲנִי יוֹדֵעַ: אַרְבַּע אִמָּהוֹת,
שְׁלֹשָׁה אָבוֹת, שְׁנֵי לֻחוֹת הַבְּרִית,
אֶחָד אֱלֹהֵינוּ שֶׁבַּשָּׁמַיִם וּבָאָרֶץ.

חֲמִשָּׁה מִי יוֹדֵעַ?

חֲמִשָּׁה אֲנִי יוֹדֵעַ: חֲמִשָּׁה חוּמְשֵׁי תוֹרָה,
אַרְבַּע אִמָּהוֹת, שְׁלֹשָׁה אָבוֹת,
שְׁנֵי לֻחוֹת הַבְּרִית,
אֶחָד אֱלֹהֵינוּ שֶׁבַּשָּׁמַיִם וּבָאָרֶץ.

שִׁשָּׁה מִי יוֹדֵעַ?

שִׁשָּׁה אֲנִי יוֹדֵעַ: שִׁשָּׁה סִדְרֵי מִשְׁנָה,
חֲמִשָּׁה חוּמְשֵׁי תוֹרָה, אַרְבַּע אִמָּהוֹת,
שְׁלֹשָׁה אָבוֹת, שְׁנֵי לֻחוֹת הַבְּרִית,
אֶחָד אֱלֹהֵינוּ שֶׁבַּשָּׁמַיִם וּבָאָרֶץ.

שִׁבְעָה מִי יוֹדֵעַ?

שִׁבְעָה אֲנִי יוֹדֵעַ: שִׁבְעָה יְמֵי שַׁבַּתָּא,
שִׁשָּׁה סִדְרֵי מִשְׁנָה, חֲמִשָּׁה חוּמְשֵׁי תוֹרָה,
אַרְבַּע אִמָּהוֹת, שְׁלֹשָׁה אָבוֹת,
שְׁנֵי לֻחוֹת הַבְּרִית,
אֶחָד אֱלֹהֵינוּ שֶׁבַּשָּׁמַיִם וּבָאָרֶץ.

שְׁמוֹנָה מִי יוֹדֵעַ?

שְׁמוֹנָה אֲנִי יוֹדֵעַ: שְׁמוֹנָה יְמֵי מִילָה,
שִׁבְעָה יְמֵי שַׁבַּתָּא, שִׁשָּׁה סִדְרֵי מִשְׁנָה,
חֲמִשָּׁה חוּמְשֵׁי תוֹרָה, אַרְבַּע אִמָּהוֹת,
שְׁלֹשָׁה אָבוֹת, שְׁנֵי לֻחוֹת הַבְּרִית,
אֶחָד אֱלֹהֵינוּ שֶׁבַּשָּׁמַיִם וּבָאָרֶץ.

Who knows one?

I know one! One is our God in heaven and earth.

Who knows two? I know two! Two are the tablets of the covenant; One is our God in heaven and earth.

Who knows three? I know three! Three are the fathers of Israel; Two are the tablets of the covenant; One is our God in heaven and earth.

Who knows four? I know four! Four are the mothers of Israel; Three are the fathers of Israel; Two are the tablets of the covenant; One is our God in heaven and earth.

Who knows five? I know five! Five are the books of the Torah; Four are the mothers of Israel; Three are the fathers of Israel; Two are the tablets of the covenant; One is our God in heaven and earth.

Who knows six? I know six! Six are the orders of the Mishnah; Five are the books of the Torah; Four are the mothers of Israel; Three are the fathers of Israel; Two are the tablets of the covenant; One is our God in heaven and earth.

Who knows seven? I know seven! Seven are the days of the week; Six are the orders of the Mishnah; Five are the books of the Torah; Four are the mothers of Israel; Three are the fathers of Israel; Two are the tablets of the covenant; One is our God in heaven and earth.

Who knows eight? I know eight! Eight are the days to circumcision; Seven are the days of the week; Six are the orders of the Mishnah; Five are the books of the Torah; Four are the mothers of Israel; Three are the fathers of Israel; Two are the tablets of the covenant; One is our God in heaven and earth.

Who knows nine? I know nine! Nine are the months to childbirth; Eight are the days to circumcision; Seven are the days of the week; Six are the orders of the Mishnah; Five are the books of the Torah; Four are the mothers of Israel; Three are the fathers of Israel; Two are the tablets of the covenant; One is our God in heaven and earth.

Who knows ten? I know ten! Ten are the commandments; Nine are the months to childbirth; Eight are the days to circumcision; Seven are the days of the week; Six are the orders of the Mishnah; Five are the books of the Torah; Four are the mothers of Israel; Three are the fathers of Israel; Two are the tablets of the covenant; One is our God in heaven and earth.

Who knows eleven? I know eleven! Eleven are the stars in Joseph's dream; Ten are the commandments; Nine are the months to childbirth; Eight are the days to circumcision; Seven are the days of the week; Six are the orders of the Mishnah; Five are the books of the Torah; Four are the mothers of Israel; Three are the fathers of Israel; Two are the tablets of the covenant; One is our God in heaven and earth.

Who knows twelve? I know twelve! Twelve are the tribes of Israel; Eleven are the stars in Joseph's dream; Ten are the commandments; Nine are the months to childbirth; Eight are the days to circumcision; Seven are the days of the week; Six are the orders of the Mishnah; Five are the books of the Torah; Four are the mothers of Israel; Three are the fathers of Israel; Two are the tablets of the covenant; One is our God in heaven and earth.

Who knows thirteen? I know thirteen! Thirteen are the attributes of God; Twelve are the tribes of Israel; Eleven are the stars in Joseph's dream; Ten are the commandments; Nine are the months to childbirth; Eight are the days to circumcision; Seven are the days of the week; Six are the orders of the Mishnah; Five are the books of the Torah; Four are the mothers of Israel; Three are the fathers of Israel; Two are the tablets of the covenant; One is our God in heaven and earth.

תִּשְׁעָה מִי יוֹדֵעַ?

תִּשְׁעָה אֲנִי יוֹדֵעַ: תִּשְׁעָה יַרְחֵי לֵדָה, שְׁמוֹנָה יְמֵי מִילָה, שִׁבְעָה יְמֵי שַׁבַּתָּא, שִׁשָּׁה סִדְרֵי מִשְׁנָה, חֲמִשָּׁה חוּמְשֵׁי תוֹרָה, אַרְבַּע אִמָּהוֹת, שְׁלֹשָׁה אָבוֹת, שְׁנֵי לֻחוֹת הַבְּרִית, אֶחָד אֱלֹהֵינוּ שֶׁבַּשָּׁמַיִם וּבָאָרֶץ.

עֲשָׂרָה מִי יוֹדֵעַ?

עֲשָׂרָה אֲנִי יוֹדֵעַ: עֲשָׂרָה דִבְּרַיָּא, תִּשְׁעָה יַרְחֵי לֵדָה, שְׁמוֹנָה יְמֵי מִילָה, שִׁבְעָה יְמֵי שַׁבַּתָּא, שִׁשָּׁה סִדְרֵי מִשְׁנָה, חֲמִשָּׁה חוּמְשֵׁי תוֹרָה, אַרְבַּע אִמָּהוֹת, שְׁלֹשָׁה אָבוֹת, שְׁנֵי לֻחוֹת הַבְּרִית, אֶחָד אֱלֹהֵינוּ שֶׁבַּשָּׁמַיִם וּבָאָרֶץ.

אַחַד עָשָׂר מִי יוֹדֵעַ?

אַחַד עָשָׂר אֲנִי יוֹדֵעַ: אַחַד עָשָׂר כּוֹכְבַיָּא, עֲשָׂרָה דִבְּרַיָּא, תִּשְׁעָה יַרְחֵי לֵדָה, שְׁמוֹנָה יְמֵי מִילָה, שִׁבְעָה יְמֵי שַׁבַּתָּא, שִׁשָּׁה סִדְרֵי מִשְׁנָה, חֲמִשָּׁה חוּמְשֵׁי תוֹרָה, אַרְבַּע אִמָּהוֹת, שְׁלֹשָׁה אָבוֹת, שְׁנֵי לֻחוֹת הַבְּרִית, אֶחָד אֱלֹהֵינוּ שֶׁבַּשָּׁמַיִם וּבָאָרֶץ.

שְׁנֵים עָשָׂר מִי יוֹדֵעַ?

שְׁנֵים עָשָׂר אֲנִי יוֹדֵעַ: שְׁנֵים עָשָׂר שִׁבְטַיָּא, אַחַד עָשָׂר כּוֹכְבַיָּא, עֲשָׂרָה דִבְּרַיָּא, תִּשְׁעָה יַרְחֵי לֵדָה, שְׁמוֹנָה יְמֵי מִילָה, שִׁבְעָה יְמֵי שַׁבַּתָּא, שִׁשָּׁה סִדְרֵי מִשְׁנָה, חֲמִשָּׁה חוּמְשֵׁי תוֹרָה, אַרְבַּע אִמָּהוֹת, שְׁלֹשָׁה אָבוֹת, שְׁנֵי לֻחוֹת הַבְּרִית, אֶחָד אֱלֹהֵינוּ שֶׁבַּשָּׁמַיִם וּבָאָרֶץ.

שְׁלֹשָׁה עָשָׂר מִי יוֹדֵעַ?

שְׁלֹשָׁה עָשָׂר אֲנִי יוֹדֵעַ: שְׁלֹשָׁה עָשָׂר מִדַּיָּא, שְׁנֵים עָשָׂר שִׁבְטַיָּא, אַחַד עָשָׂר כּוֹכְבַיָּא, עֲשָׂרָה דִבְּרַיָּא, תִּשְׁעָה יַרְחֵי לֵדָה, שְׁמוֹנָה יְמֵי מִילָה, שִׁבְעָה יְמֵי שַׁבַּתָּא, שִׁשָּׁה סִדְרֵי מִשְׁנָה, חֲמִשָּׁה חוּמְשֵׁי תוֹרָה, אַרְבַּע אִמָּהוֹת, שְׁלֹשָׁה אָבוֹת, שְׁנֵי לֻחוֹת הַבְּרִית, אֶחָד אֱלֹהֵינוּ שֶׁבַּשָּׁמַיִם וּבָאָרֶץ.

That Father bought for two zuzim; **One kid, one kid.**

The cat came and ate the kid

That father bought for two zuzim; **One kid, one kid.**

The dog came and bit the cat that ate the kid

That father bought for two zuzim; **One kid, one kid.**

The stick came and beat the dog that bit the cat that ate the kid

That father bought for two zuzim; **One kid, one kid.**

The fire came and burned the stick that beat the dog that bit the cat that ate the kid

That father bought for two zuzim; **One kid, one kid.**

The water came and quenched the fire that burned the stick that beat the dog that bit the cat that ate the kid

That father bought for two zuzim; **One kid, one kid.**

The ox came and drank the water that quenched the fire that burned the stick that beat the dog that bit the cat that ate the kid

That father bought for two zuzim; **One kid, one kid.**

The slaughterer came and killed the ox that drank the water that quenched the fire that burned the stick that beat the dog that bit the cat that ate the kid

That father bought for two zuzim; **One kid, one kid.**

The angel of death came and slew the slaughterer that killed the ox that drank the water that quenched the fire that burned the stick that beat the dog that bit the cat that ate the kid

That father bought for two zuzim; **One kid, one kid.**

The Holy One, blessed be He, came and slew the angel of death that slew the slaughterer that killed the ox that drank the water that quenched the fire that burned the stick that beat the dog that bit the cat that ate the kid

That father bought for two zuzim; **One kid, one kid.**

דְּזַבִּין אַבָּא בִּתְרֵי זוּזֵי, **חַד גַּדְיָא, חַד גַּדְיָא.**

וְאָתָא שׁוּנְרָא, וְאָכְלָה לְגַדְיָא,

דְּזַבִּין אַבָּא בִּתְרֵי זוּזֵי, **חַד גַּדְיָא, חַד גַּדְיָא.**

וְאָתָא כַלְבָּא, וְנָשַׁךְ לְשׁוּנְרָא, דְּאָכְלָה לְגַדְיָא,

דְּזַבִּין אַבָּא בִּתְרֵי זוּזֵי, **חַד גַּדְיָא, חַד גַּדְיָא.**

וְאָתָא חוּטְרָא, וְהִכָּה לְכַלְבָּא, דְּנָשַׁךְ לְשׁוּנְרָא, דְּאָכְלָה לְגַדְיָא,

דְּזַבִּין אַבָּא בִּתְרֵי זוּזֵי, **חַד גַּדְיָא, חַד גַּדְיָא.**

וְאָתָא נוּרָא, וְשָׂרַף לְחוּטְרָא, דְּהִכָּה לְכַלְבָּא, דְּנָשַׁךְ לְשׁוּנְרָא, דְּאָכְלָה לְגַדְיָא,

דְּזַבִּין אַבָּא בִּתְרֵי זוּזֵי, **חַד גַּדְיָא, חַד גַּדְיָא**

וְאָתָא מַיָּא, וְכָבָה לְנוּרָא,

דְּשָׂרַף לְחוּטְרָא, דְּהִכָּה לְכַלְבָּא

דְּנָשַׁךְ לְשׁוּנְרָא, דְּאָכְלָה לְגַדְיָא,

דְּזַבִּין אַבָּא בִּתְרֵי זוּזֵי, **חַד גַּדְיָא, חַד גַּדְיָא.**

וְאָתָא תוֹרָא, וְשָׁתָא לְמַיָּא, דְּכָבָה לְנוּרָא, דְּשָׂרַף לְחוּטְרָא, דְּהִכָּה לְכַלְבָּא, דְּנָשַׁךְ לְשׁוּנְרָא, דְּאָכְלָה לְגַדְיָא,

דְּזַבִּין אַבָּא בִּתְרֵי זוּזֵי, **חַד גַּדְיָא, חַד גַּדְיָא.**

וְאָתָא הַשּׁוֹחֵט, וְשָׁחַט לְתוֹרָא, דְּשָׁתָא לְמַיָּא, דְּכָבָה לְנוּרָא, דְּשָׂרַף לְחוּטְרָא, דְּהִכָּה לְכַלְבָּא, דְּנָשַׁךְ לְשׁוּנְרָא, דְּאָכְלָה לְגַדְיָא,

דְּזַבִּין אַבָּא בִּתְרֵי זוּזֵי, **חַד גַּדְיָא, חַד גַּדְיָא.**

וְאָתָא מַלְאַךְ הַמָּוֶת, וְשָׁחַט לְשׁוֹחֵט, דְּשָׁחַט לְתוֹרָא, דְּשָׁתָא לְמַיָּא, דְּכָבָה לְנוּרָא, דְּשָׂרַף לְחוּטְרָא, דְּהִכָּה לְכַלְבָּא, דְּנָשַׁךְ לְשׁוּנְרָא, דְּאָכְלָה לְגַדְיָא,

דְּזַבִּין אַבָּא בִּתְרֵי זוּזֵי, **חַד גַּדְיָא, חַד גַּדְיָא.**

וְאָתָא הַקָּדוֹשׁ בָּרוּךְ הוּא, וְשָׁחַט לְמַלְאַךְ הַמָּוֶת, דְּשָׁחַט לְתוֹרָא, דְּשָׁתָא לְמַיָּא, דְּכָבָה לְנוּרָא, דְּשָׂרַף לְחוּטְרָא, דְּהִכָּה לְכַלְבָּא, דְּנָשַׁךְ לְשׁוּנְרָא, דְּאָכְלָה לְגַדְיָא,

דְּזַבִּין אַבָּא בִּתְרֵי זוּזֵי, **חַד גַּדְיָא, חַד גַּדְיָא.**

www.hrhaggadah.com

The website delves into human rights issues currently affecting Israel and the Jewish community to help us better understand both our own views and the views of those who disagree with us.

Visit or scan to continue the conversation.